PSYCHOTHERAPY AND CULTURE

PSYCHOTHERAPY AND CULTURE

Weaving Inner and Outer Worlds

Zack Eleftheriadou

KARNAC

First published in 2010 by
Karnac Books Ltd
118 Finchley Road, London NW3 5HT

British Library Cataloguing in Publication Data

A C.I.P. for this book is available from the British Library

ISBN: 978 1 85575 625 0

Edited, designed and produced by The Studio Publishing Services Ltd
www.publishingservicesuk.co.uk
e-mail: studio@publishingservicesuk.co.uk

Printed in Great Britain

www.karnacbooks.com

CONTENTS

ACKNOWLEDGEMENTS

This book was a result of a long journey. I am absolutely thrilled and indebted to so many people for its completion. I would like to extend my heartfelt thanks to my dear colleagues: Dr Aileen Alleyne, Lourdes Bedrasco, Professor Brett Kahr, Professor Alessandra Lemma, Professor Zenobia Nadirshaw, Professor Stephen Palmer, Antonis Sigalas, and Dr Susan Strauss, who have always been available for professional questions and for all their support and creative ideas on different aspects of therapy and cross-cultural work throughout the years and this book. I would also like to extend a huge thanks to Dr Felicity Dirmeik, who has shown such generosity in supporting me to understand life and its intricate meanings. To Anne Horne, who has taught me a vast amount about children's worlds, and I have gained so much from her lively engagement and clarity of independent psychoanalytic thinking. I particularly thank her for her kindness over the years. To my dear supervisor, Dr Catriona Hood, thanks for all the ideas you shared with me; your excellent clinical judgement and astuteness are so very much missed. I feel indebted to Jafar Kareem who invited me to join the team at NAFSIYAT all those years ago and Lennox Thomas who gave me the wonderful opportunity to become the 'Co-ordinator of the Child and Family referrals' there. I learnt a huge amount from both of them and I value the professional network we developed. Additionally, my 4 years at the Medical Foundation for the Care of Victims of Torture, working with unaccompanied adolescents, will always stay with me, as well as the very special people I worked with there. I have to warmly thank the guest authors for agreeing to be part of this ambitious project from its conception. They have produced excellent contributions and such patience with the fine-tuning of their chapters. I have appreciated your engagement and it certainly has made cross-cultural work less lonely—I hope we can continue to think together about the issues. I would like to say a big thanks to Martyn for always being positive with the amount of work and deadlines I had to fulfil, and for such careful typing and comments. Also, of course, many thanks to the Karnac staff, especially Lucy Shirley, for a very smooth editing and publication process. To PC, words are not quite enough to express my gratitude for your constancy and encouragement to put my ideas on paper, for making time for me to write and for dealing with all the IT stuff that I couldn't make sense of. To JCC, AGC, and SMC for all your challenging questions and beautifully detailed and unique observations on life and how things work. Writing a book like this, one inevitably goes on many "psychological homeland" visits. I feel I have learnt a colossal amount throughout the writing and it has been a remarkable psychological exploration of my roots and the various cultures I now embrace. To Mihalakis and Maria, thanks for all the wonderful memories, and to Theano for being a wonderful story teller; all three of you have been significant protagonists during a very significant time of my life. To all my dear friends for their patience with my preoccupation with the writing, and I am so glad you kept me in the loop with what really matters.

My sincere thanks to Sage for their kind permission to reprint the following:

Chapter Three contains the case of "Angela", originally published in Eleftheriadou, Z. (1997). Cultural differences in the therapeutic process. In: I. Horton & V. Verma (Eds.), *The Needs of Counsellors and Psychotherapists* (pp. 69–83). London: Sage.

Chapter Five contains pp. 71–73 from the chapter, Eleftheriadou, Z. (1997). Cultural differences in the therapeutic process. In: I. Horton & V. Verma (Eds.), *The Needs of Counsellors and Psychotherapists* (pp. 69–83). London: Sage.

Chapter Six has some writings incorporated from Eleftheriadou, Z. (1997). Cultural differences in the therapeutic process. In: I. Horton & V. Verma (Eds.), *The Needs of Counsellors and Psychotherapists* (pp. 69–83). London: Sage.

Chapter Six includes the expanded case of "Alessandro", originally published in Eleftheriadou, Z. (2003). Cross-cultural counselling psychology. In: R. Woolfe, W. Dryden, & S. Strawbridge (Eds.), *Handbook of Counselling Psychology* (2nd edn) (pp. 55–517). London: Sage.

Chapter Seven is an expanded and amended version of Eleftheriadou, Z. (1999). Assessing the counselling needs of ethnic minorities in Britain, originally published in P. Laungani & S. Palmer (Eds.), *Counselling in a Multicultural Society* (pp. 113–132). London: Sage.

Chapter Nine, written by Edino Dzeko, was adapted from the MSc In Counselling Psychology thesis, entitled: *Images of Exile: a Qualitative Study of Refugees' Stories*, under the supervision of Dr Goodrich, for the Department of Psychology, University of East London, 2001.

Chapter Ten is a reprint of Eleftheriadou, Z. (1999). Psychotherapeutic work with refugees: understanding the therapist's countertransference. Originally published in *Psychodynamic Counselling*, 5(2): 219–230.

Finally, and perhaps most importantly, my heartfelt thanks to my clients and students over the years. I could not write such a text without you, and I have respected your trust in our therapeutic/ supervisory relationship. I have learnt from you more about life than any theory can provide, and I feel extremely privileged.

ABOUT THE AUTHORS

Aileen Alleyne is a UKCP registered psychodynamic psychotherapist and clinical supervisor in private practice. She is a full member of FIP, BACP, and Nafsiyat Intercultural Therapy Centre. Alongside her private practice, she consults to organizations on issues of difference and diversity within various work settings, such as the NHS, Social Services, Education, and the Metropolitan Police. Her academic career has included lectureships at several London colleges and universities, including Goldsmiths' College, University of London, for a continuous period of eight years. Aileen's doctoral research, examining black and Asian workers' experiences in three institutional settings, highlights the concept of "the internal oppressor". It offers ways of deepening understanding of black and minority ethnic people's psychological reactions to the negative impact of racism. Aileen is the author of several book chapters and journal papers exploring themes on black–white dynamics, shame, and black identity wounding. (www.aileenalleyne.com)

Beverley Costa was born in London and raised in a bicultural family surrounded by various languages and religions. Her father was Greek Cypriot and her mother was the daughter of Polish–Russian refugees. After training as a group and individual psychotherapist and psychodramatist, she worked in a multi-cultural educational organization in Reading. During this time, she encountered many people trying to cope with distressing situations with no appropriate outlet for expression. Beverley is the Director of Mothertongue, a culturally sensitive therapeutic support service for people from black and minority ethnic communities, which she founded in 2000. In 2007, Mothertongue won the National Charity Awards, in 2008, the Award for Excellence in the Practice of Counselling and Psychotherapy from the British Association for Counselling and Psychotherapy (BACP) and in 2009 received the Queen's Award for Voluntary Service. beverley@mothertongue.org.uk; www.mothertongue.org.uk

Zack Eleftheriadou was born in Famagusta, Cyprus. After the war in 1974, she moved to Jeddah, Saudi Arabia and then to London, UK. She holds an MSc in Child Development, MA in the Psychology of Therapy and Counselling, Diploma in Eating Disorders (NCfED), Diploma Infant Mental Health, is a HPC Registered Psychologist (BPS Chartered Counselling Psychologist and a Chartered Scientist and a member of the BPS 'Register of Applied Psychology Practice Supervisors'), as well as an integrative psychotherapist, a psychoanalytic psychotherapist (UKCP registered), Professional Member of BACP, Regent's College, School of Psychotherapy and Counselling and Nafsiyat: the Intercultural Therapy Centre (London). She has lectured since 1990 and has written extensively in the area of cross-cultural work/refugees, including the book *Transcultural Counselling* (1994). She has a private practice in North London, working clinically with children, families and adults and supervising students. She has worked as a visiting lecturer/consultant at the Tavistock Clinic, The Anna Freud Clinic, The British Association for Psychotherapists, Universities of Hertfordshire, Middlesex, City, East London, Surrey and University College London, among others. She is ex-Chair of the BAC Division 'RACE'. She is thesis reader, a Psychotherapist for the School of Life (London) and Patron for Mothertongue, the Multi-Ethnic Counselling and Listening Service (Reading).

Edina Dzeko was born and grew up in Sarajevo, Bosnia. She came to London at the age of twenty-one as a refugee, following the outbreak of the war in her country. She later trained as a counselling psychologist and is currently working within Hertfordshire Partnership Foundation NHS Trust. Her areas of interest are trauma and refugees, and she has worked with clients who present with dissociative personalities resulting from severe childhood trauma. She also incorporates energy psychology methods in her work with clients.

PREFACE

About twenty years ago, as I was beginning to venture into a psychology career, I was asked to lecture at an American International University on the subject of cross-cultural psychology. The whole experience was as an eye-opener, and, after extensive research, I realized I could find only a few books on the "role" of culture in psychology and psychotherapy. It became apparent that I had to look beyond the subjects of general psychology and psychotherapy, such as sociology, social psychology, and anthropology. This became the start of the most fascinating journey in teaching, clinical and consultancy work, and, of course, my own personal development in the cross-cultural arena.

During my various trainings in psychology and psychotherapy, cross-cultural issues were generally not explored in depth, but my own background (being a Greek-Cypriot who had lived in other countries) and the fact that I had studied in Cypriot, Greek, American, and British schools provided me some significant "tools" which helped me to relate and understand my international students, colleagues, and clients. I am aware that I hold a strong belief for social justice, identify with the deprived or politically persecuted, inevitably connected to my own experience of becoming a refugee, losing everything, and having to start from scratch—literally. This has always made it easier for me to identify with those who are not mainstream, those struggling with higher levels of frustration, anxiety, and deprivation. This has been reflected in my professional choices of working in many deprived areas of London.

I live among an extremely multi-cultural group of colleagues, family, and friends in which one can take the "mixedness" for granted. It is only when I leave multi-cultural London that I am often reminded of how different my reality is. The whole cross-cultural voyage has been a long one, and writing this book has certainly been both fulfilling and cathartic. The process has been one of drawing from inwards to the professional, alongside many clinical and teaching exchanges with clients and students from all types of backgrounds. Similar to my own process, in order for my students to really grasp cross-cultural issues, they would have to engage both academically and emotionally. Taking this on board early on, I adapted the teaching methods completely. I now strongly believe that teaching cross-cultural psychology has to be experiential and theoretical, concurrently. In my clinical practice and supervision of students' work, I have been aware that my clients required acknowledgement of cross-cultural issues, in order to make a connection. I am now convinced that the more I was able to hear the cultural issues in my clients' material, the more the material "flowed" and we were able to work on a much deeper level, which is more fulfilling for both parties.

The tone of the book will undoubtedly reflect my own European and Middle Eastern homes and my cross-cultural relationships. I cannot but reflect on what I have been exposed to personally and professionally through my experiences. In this book I have drawn primarily from the "stories" of my clients and students. (All of the identities of any clients and students mentioned in the text have been disguised to retain anonymity. At times, identifying characteristics have been altered, or several clients' backgrounds have been merged to ensure anonymity. Through this writing style, I strongly believe the essential learning points on cross-cultural work remain, without compromising any personal details of any of our clients and students. The exception is Chapter Ten, where the respondents agreed to have their stories shared for learning purposes, but retain anonymity.) Despite (and inevitably) using my own socialization influences, I hope that I can demonstrate a way of truly engaging with the differences, barriers as well as the similarities.

Aims of the book

This book is a selection of readings that focus on cross-cultural relationships and examines how culture and racial factors manifest in the clinical setting. For the purposes of this book, the main focus will be the psychological journey in the background of this rich and vast cultural context. In other words, we will examine how the socio-political is made sense of within the psychological sphere. The aim is to understand the dynamic interaction between the person, the familial, and the cultural system, as well as the socio-cultural context of the therapy. These dynamics will be examined throughout the text, using case material from specific populations, stemming from the all of the authors' extensive clinical experience. Inevitably, this implies that it was beyond the scope of this book to include clients from a wider range of cultural and racial backgrounds, but it would not have done justice to them, as this area is simply too vast. My hope is that the clinical examples challenge the myth that people of different cultures do not need or use therapy, and also show that if the therapy offered is respectful of them as a person and their culture, they will engage in longer term, psychotherapeutic work.

One of the main aims of this text is to open up a discussion about how to work with both cross-cultural differentiation and integration (Pedersen, 1997). I hope the ideas presented in the book will be useful to all of us who work with people from different social contexts; such as class differences, language, sexuality, age, among many others. It is not the aim to present a new kind of theoretical model (since we have far too many already) or a "how to do it", which is fit only for those who are culturally or racially different, as this would suggest that "they need something which is different". I hope the ideas presented engage professionals belonging to any professional home and that it encourages further discussion of cross-cultural issues.

Many names have been to describe the field of cross-cultural work, such as multi-cultural counselling, intercultural therapy, but the name mainly used in this text will be "transcultural" (see Eleftheriadou, 1994). In this context, "transcultural" is used to describe what happens when two people come together from different value systems and try to create a connection. As in my previous writings,

> "cross-cultural" implies that we go across or "inter" culture in try-
> ing to understand another person. That is, we use our own refer-
> ence system to understand the client's experience rather than going
> beyond our own worldview. The difference between cross-cultural
> and transcultural is a crucial one because "trans" denotes that
> counsellors need to work beyond their cultural differences. [*ibid.*,
> p. 31]

I believe that a cross-cultural interaction can transcend barriers and be a real human meeting, although we have to work harder to understand the potential "barriers". We need to become more culturally responsive therapists, viewing the person as a whole, and taking into account how the socio-cultural factors contribute to the formation of the self and relationships with others.

I would urge the reader to keep in mind that these writings are based within a particular time frame and context (bearing in mind, it is written from the experience of multi-culturalism [mainly] in the London/Reading, UK context as the professional base), and this book is a response to this particular point in time. As a clinician, I do not claim to overcome all barriers, but, as a result of my experience, I do hold a great deal of hope that the majority of the time we can find *enough common ground* to connect together well. Throughout the text, relevant references to theoretical and research material will be given, although the focus is primarily an applied one. This is because, as Steiner states,

> theory may in fact obstruct the analyst's capacity to open himself to
> the patient's material. Perhaps such disappointment with theory is
> a healthy state of affairs and leaves us aware that a good theory is
> a fine servant but a poor master. [1996, p. 1082]

Although there is a strong psychoanalytic strand throughout the book, I do not believe this is the only framework to understand human nature or to follow as a clinician, and taking more than one framework is, in itself, a cross-cultural exercise. There are useful ideas that I refer to, but the emphasis is a flexible framework, hence, the book includes two chapters which do not necessarily follow this theoretical school of thought. My own professional background, in a way, also reflects the travels between different theoretical frameworks, as my own training began through a psychology degree, which I believe provided me with a kind of "methodology" in my personal and professional constant search for meaning. The word "methodology" does not in any way imply a strictly scientifically rigorous way, but a structure for observing and openness for the kinds of factors that require consideration. Later, I trained in integrative, existential/phenomenological psychotherapy, and later still completed a training in psychoanalytic psychotherapy, and have taken an active role in encouraging therapists to take social responsibility for their work.

I have worked with a range of backgrounds and age groups: adults, adolescents, children, and infants. The former have taught me about narratives and the way we engage and create meanings out of our life experiences. The latter groups have taught me about the power of the non-verbal, which links in to my early influences with Paddington Green Child Psychiatry. There, I was introduced to the work of one of the most creative theorists in psychoanalysis, D. W. Winnicott. Many of the ideas in the book reflect this influence.

Culture is defined in a particular way in this book, recognizing that there are cultural practices that are helpful and enriching to our clients and others that are simply power relations and inequalities enforced on the individual, on men, women, and children. Furthermore, I believe that some cultural practices and rites are simply brutal. Additionally, we can explore cultural elements in relation to our clients, but we cannot take on the whole culture, it is *only our clients' culture* that helps us to work with them and understand their meanings. There are elements we may not understand, or agree with, but we have to pace our client's exploration and not impose our western values on them. However, there may be practices that are illegal in our cultural context, and one has to have an open conversation with the client from the outset about the way forward if we are to work together, clearly outlining the legal issues. These issues are extremely delicate and sometimes unfold in rather unclear ways clinically. Although there are many different books

being published frequently in the cross-cultural psychology /
therapy discipline, the aim of this book provides a way to integrate
the issues into our clinical work rather than place them in a separate field.

The racial and cultural differences and bridges are emphasized,
but there is also a need to hold on to the individuality of the person and ensure that this does not get lost at any cost. I strongly hope
that the reader is able to apply all the theoretical and clinical ideas
to working with any client. It is a way of helping us to become sensitive to the differences and the importance of the social context,
cultural and racial roots, and, subsequently, the formation of our
complex and ever changing psycho-social identity. At the risk of
sounding rather "traditional" or even nostalgic, I really do believe
that in recent times, with much global movement and change, it has
become *even more* significant for people to hold on to a sense of feeling rooted. I must add that I am referring to the individual's "comfort levels" and not prescriptive political views on how they should
belong to the new culture.

In focusing on race and cultural issues, I am aware that other
highly significant social factors, such as class and gender, are not
explored in great detail, but feel that there are extensive writings
and research on these (e.g., Altman, 1995; Wheeler, 2006), and my
personal belief is that the most neglected (still) are the issues of race
and culture; hence, the focus of this book. In fact, in many writings
and workshops I have attended over the years, they are examined
together. Here, it is the intention to study cross-cultural issues
closely without diluting them with other "social" factors and influences, even if there is overlap.

Throughout the book (apart from guest authors' chapters, where
they clarify their own terminology), I will be referring to the consulting room process as "therapy" for shorthand, unless I intend to
refer to the separate fields of counselling and psychotherapy. It is
also important to say a word about what is psychotherapy at this
stage: the whole word "psychotherapy", comes from "psycho",
which stems from the Greek word "psyche", or the healing of the
human soul, mind, breath of life. The latter part, "therapy", stems
from "tharapeia", meaning, finding the remedy or treatment
to health problems. In the mental health profession, it is a dynamic,
in-depth conscious and unconscious process that explores and

analyses the person's life, behaviours, and cognitive processes and attributed meanings. It is a relational process where therapist and client work together to "co-construct" (Stern, 2004) meanings, the therapist being a professional and expert in their profession, but not on the client's life.

Chapter One is entitled "Introduction" and provides an overview of the issues and makes the case for why another textbook in this field is necessary. It makes explicit the backdrop of my philosophy and motives for writing a cross-cultural text. The central aim is to weave the cultural/racial layer into our theoretical thinking and clinical work. The overriding belief is that learning needs to be applied, rather than merely theoretical, since we know that:

> For most people, prejudice is too deeply rooted in their own belief systems, is too consistent with their day-today behavior, and receives too much support and encouragement from the people around them to be reduced by a book, a film or a radio broadcast. [Aronson, 1984, pp. 259–260]

Chapter Two is entitled "Culture, race, and identity: meanings and complexities". This chapter explores the different concepts of culture, race, and identity, and demonstrates how they are socially and politically constructed, but also how people themselves may identify with these. Every culture has implicit and explicit ideas on different ag-related norms and expectations. Whether these are adhered to or are rejected at some stage, they will have an influence on how the personality or relationships are shaped. Furthermore, throughout the life cycle, there are multiple cultural and racial influences that contribute to a person's psycho-cultural and racial identity.

As Tuckwell reminds us,

> Race and culture are multi-layered concepts that embrace sociological, political and psychological perspectives. Both constructs are highly significant in the interplay between outer world experiences and internalized beliefs about self and others, and in this way they have similar attributes to social organization and identity. [2006, p. 143]

Chapter Three, "Pre-transference, transference, and counter-transference" introduces these psychodynamic concepts early in the book, as they are thought to be extremely useful in clinical work. They can inform us of the unspoken, often unconscious, aspects of the communication, which may not emerge for some time. This chapter emphasizes that this type of in-depth interaction can only take place by monitoring our own conscious and unconscious reactions to our clients.

The next chapter, Four, is entitled "Barriers to cross-cultural work", as a way of outlining some of the most common barriers to cross-cultural communication. Our work is full of potential communication frustrations and misunderstandings, but becoming aware of them can deepen the communication and make the client feel there is hope of being understood or "emotionally met" by the therapist.

Chapter Five is entitled "Clinical assessment", which warrants a separate chapter in order to emphasize the significance of the first contact or first meetings with the client. Taking a proper psycho-social history is essential when taking on a new client, but also, if the initial contact is successful, it gives clients hope of being understood and supported in some way.

In Chapter Six, entitled "The therapeutic relationship", introduces concepts such as the therapeutic alliance, holding, and containment are utilized to think about how the two parties, the client and the therapist, engage in clinical work. It is perceived as an exploratory process, in that, as therapists, we have the theoretical and clinical knowledge, but we are guided by the client's communications and emotional state as to which direction the therapy goes. This chapter demonstrates that we can keep a balance, not to retreat into the internal world or to focus on the external world and to keep in mind the potential relationship between the two.

The next chapter, Chapter Seven, is entitled "The psycho-social experiences of different immigrant groups and the multi-faceted migration journey". The aim is to help us understand different psycho-social experiences and how they contribute to people's thinking and conscious and unconscious behaviours. This chapter is by no means conclusive regarding what people bring, but indicates their different psycho-social needs. The migration journey is discussed at length, to illustrate that it is a long process and may take many convoluted turns. The person's inner resources, as well as the external environment, are contributing factors in how people settle in a new country.

Chapter Eight, entitled "A working model of a community based, culturally sensitive counselling service", is written by the Director of Mothertongue, Beverley Costa. In this chapter, we are introduced to a counselling service that successfully meets the needs of BME groups and has developed ways to reach out to the local community. The local community and the service maintain an ongoing dialogue that identifies the client needs.

In order to get to grips with cross-cultural dynamics, it is important to gather material from clinical and non-clinical populations, as the former cannot possibly be representative of Black Minority Ethnic (BME) populations in any way. All the above chapters have focused mainly on clinical populations, but the next chapter, Nine, entitled "The stories of four Bosnian women", contributed by Edina Dzeko, is a moving account of four Bosnian women and their journey and perceptions on losing their homeland and moving to the UK. The women simply told their stories to the interviewer, without therapeutic comment and their stories are recorded here as an insight into their journeys.

Chapter Ten is entitled "Psychotherapeutic work with refugees: understanding the therapist's countertransference", and examines the specific unconscious reactions we may experience when working with refugees or exiles. It builds on the previous chapter, and Chapter Three, to highlight the unique dynamics in the clinical encounter when working with this particular group of clients.

Chapter Eleven is entitled "Psychodynamic considerations for diversity consultancy in organizations", by Aileen Alleyne. Aileen writes from a consultant's perspective of the conscious and unconscious dynamics when working with organizational groups. Whether we work in an organization or in private practice, it gives us a detailed account of some of the defences that come into play alongside racial factors.

Readership

This book is aimed towards both trainee and experienced psychologists, counsellors, psychotherapists, social workers, and other mental health workers who are interested in enhancing their cross-cultural therapeutic work.

References

Aronson, E. (1984). *The Social Animal*. New York: Freeman.

Pedersen, P. (1997). *Culture-Centered Counseling Interventions*. Thousand Oaks, CA: Sage.

Eleftheriadou, Z. (1994). *Transcultural Counselling*. London: Central Books.

Steiner, J. (1996). The aim of psychoanalysis in theory and practice. *International Journal of Psychoanalysis, 77*: 1073–1083.

Stern, D. N. (2004). *The Present Moment in Psychotherapy and Everyday Life*. New York: W. W. Norton.

Tuckwell, G. (2006). Psychodynamic counselling, "race" and culture. In: S. Wheeler (Ed.), *Difference and Diversity in Counselling* (pp. 137–155). New York: Palgrave.

CHAPTER ONE

Introduction

Zack Eleftheriadou

This chapter introduces the wider socio-political context, including multi-culturalism issues, and outlines the reasons why the needs of Black Minority Ethnic (BME) populations have not adequately been met within the mental health services. It also aims to provide an overview of the relationship between culture and psychiatry. Although the focus of this book is on those clients who attend counselling and therapeutic support, a significant proportion of BME clients will have had some link with the psychiatric services.

The wider socio-political context

The world we live in has become pluralized, culturally, racially, and religiously. When different cultures come into contact, it can sometimes be explosive, as different regions/individuals have such different levels of tolerance and expectations. Multi-culturalism has a long history, in how countries have negotiated their differences and similarities. Generally, increasing communication and travel have improved international communication, which is evident in many educational and professional spheres. We have seen both sides of the spectrum, events that have pushed us into peace and increased communication, and others into war, forcing us into alienation. Therefore, multi-cultural work and research are not always positive, helpful, or even successful because of misunderstandings of cross-cultural behaviour and values. Nowadays, there are still remnants of some old, colonial types of thinking. If we just pay attention to the language used to explain differences, it quickly becomes evident how the words reflect the political arena; for example, terms such as "Third World" have their own negative connotations and are still used in some contexts. All these experiences are emotionally powerful and (often) have a lasting impact on people's psyches. Although we try to keep the fear of the unknown and unfamiliar at bay, it often becomes distorted and can reach the destructive divide, such as the disturbing events we are faced with historically and currently "in the name of religion". Of course, this fear can be located in all of us, but we like to think it is located in the "other".

People go through dramatic measures to find a sense of belonging (even if this is a somewhat transient phase), either going through the process of separating themselves or creating new sub-cultures and languages/dialects. Sadly, hardly a week goes by where a controversial cultural or racial issue is not in the news, be it Muslim girls wearing the headscarf in western countries or Christians wearing a cross at work in Britain, a religious leader making suggestions of how to incorporate cultural issues, or whether migrants should really be allowed to become British residents. These are only some of the stories making the headlines in London, during February 2008 (I would urge the reader to follow the news headlines systematically for a short period of time, as it is quite an interesting exercise to note what and how events are reported).

There are never "clear" pathways to follow or, indeed, answers to these political questions, and they can really throw the public into despair, with a feeling that there are no cultural bridges. There is simply no other way but to struggle with these issues, with difficult questions, such as how much should people be allowed to portray their identity (race, culture, and religion), and at which point does it become unacceptable or offensive to others. The boundaries are not clear, but we try to create clarity through rules and new laws. Some would argue that in most cities, such as London, most of us live in a minority culture, be it culturally or religiously.

Mental health services and ethnic minorities

Even to this day it is true to say that the cross-cultural field remains an "outsider" and one that the mental health field has been uncertain whether to invite in as a long-lost relative or to treat it as an uninvited guest that keeps challenging the status quo. To summarize, the following issues still remain problematic, as identified by clinicians and researchers (Bhugra & Bhui, 2006, Dalal, 2006; Fernando, 1995, Laungani, 2002, National Institute for Mental Health in England (NIMHE), 2003):

- ethnic minorities are less likely to receive talking therapies and are more likely to be referred to specialist services, usually psychiatric services;
- not all therapists have wanted to, or felt confidently skilled to, really engage with minority issues;
- there are still considerably fewer therapists of BME backgrounds;
- due to fewer BME staff, there is greater racism, and when BME clients complain about racism, it is often dismissed as it is not part of their internal or external experience;
- because psychotherapy has been a private, closed world, it is difficult to know what really happens to race and culture within psychotherapy;
- there is still a myth that ethnic minorities are not capable of self-reflection and that they do not need counselling or psychotherapy;
- there is still a lack of culturally aware, skilled therapists who are willing to grapple with these issues, and language barriers remain problematic;
- there is subtle discrimination in all of us which manifests at an institutional level (see Chapter Eleven in this text for exploration of these issues);

- theories have focused on individual psychic identity development, rather than the family, group or culture. Also, existing texts on mental health across cultures have tended to concentrate on the most "obvious" or "concrete" differences;
- we fall into either ignoring cultural differences or over-generalizing, which often results in stereotyping clients;
- there are inevitably economic issues, in that low-cost therapy is not readily available for diverse communities.

The relationship between BME communities and mental health is a difficult one, and yet this is very much the reality in Britain today (Fernando & Keating, 2008). Ethnocentricism and racist perceptions have played a large part in misdiagnosis and over-diagnosis of BME populations in psychiatry. Littlewood and Lipsedge (1989) demonstrated clearly in their seminal text, entitled *Aliens and Alienists,* how racial and cultural dynamics not only complicate the factors one needs to take into account, but would often lead to over-diagnoses of mental disorders according to the psychiatric (*DSM*) categories. Consequently, medication would be prescribed more often, and when it was prescribed it would be higher than for those who belong to the majority culture. The evidence provided was alarming, and created a dramatic challenge to all of the mental health services, particularly those who are in the powerful role of diagnosing people who experience mental distress (evidence is backed by Fernando, 1995).

According to Bhugra and Bhui: "it is more likely that psychotherapy services are not accessible to individuals from ethnic minorities because of physical and psychological barriers erected by the service providers" (2006, p. 53). In general, black people especially have been seen to be "inferior" and "somehow out of control", "mad" and "bad". As a result, there has been a close relationship with forensic psychiatry and ethnic minorities, demonstrating that the fear of black people is often acted upon by giving them a more difficult time through the court system; for example, it is less likely that black defendants will be granted bail than white defendants (Fernando, Ndegwa, & Wilson, 1998; Hawkes, 1999). Furthermore, many of the clients referred into the mental health services live in what would be considered a socio-economically deprived area. It is not by any means the experience of all, but many ethnic minorities tend to reside in poorer areas, which is reflected in every facility, including educational facilities. They experience higher degrees of crime, unemployment (or, if they do find work, it tends to be of a low income), racism, and generally suffer from what Altman (1995) refers to as "more than the usual doses of anger, fear and despair" (p. 1).

Every culture has a concept of mental illness and a related one on mental health. All societies have ways of dealing with what is "undesirable" behaviour and specific places to which people go. In some societies, the appropriate way to deal with distress is to visit a shrine; in others, it is the therapy consulting room. It is often not clear what is psychiatrically abnormal and what is socially abnormal or "eccentric", even within another culture. It is interesting to note that often those who have mental health problems are dismissed as crazy and senseless. Yet,

> mentally ill individuals do not always invent their own system of symbolic communication: they often employ the dominant system which others use—but they are likely to do so in a way which to others seem inconvenient and clumsy. [Littlewood & Lipsedge, 1989, p. 220]

The socio-political context of therapy

There is now increasing recognition (although this is by no means held by all theoretical schools of thought) that the disciplines of counselling and psychotherapy have their own socio-political contexts. To some extent, it is inevitable that any theoretical concepts will reflect the values of the originators. For example, one does not have to dig deep to realize that psychoanalysis arose out of a particular context; it was created from the lives of Jewish people in Europe during the Holocaust. Many of the ideas presented in the book have been taken from psychoanalysis, so it is worth outlining some issues that have arisen within this field. Most writings in psychoanalysis have been on anti-Semitism, and yet there is very little on racism in a broader sense. There seem to be many therapists from culturally diverse, but not varied, racial backgrounds (very few are able to train in therapy, particularly on the longer and more intensive trainings, which are, of course, more costly). Perhaps for this very reason it is too painful to be explicit about personal experiences. Also, as many believe, events like the Holocaust and its impact have been so shocking that survivors have not been able to verbalize it, but the next generation has had (or perhaps is, slowly) to find words to do so. The founder of psychoanalysis, Sigmund Freud, who was himself an exile, stated that "it is precisely the minor differences in people who are otherwise alike that form the basis of feelings of strangeness and hostility between them (1918a, p. 199).

Psychoanalysis has, of course, been applied to different cultures, but as a system in itself, not one that has to consider what culture might mean, how it affects an individual and group, both consciously and unconsciously. Culture has been viewed as a screen, a defence, and very much belonging to the "external" world as opposed to the "internal". Until recently, few writers have been interested to discover the manifestations of cultural material into the unconscious. Psychoanalysis has so many useful concepts that we can utilize, but also could incorporate the social context more.

As Moodley and Palmer (2006) say:

> The challenge for psychotherapy is to engage psychoanalytic theory in an innovative and alternative way so that the notions of multiple-identities and multiple selves begin to evolve new epistemologies in research as well as in the actual delivery of psychotherapy. At the same time the traditional ideas that encompass race, culture and ethnicity, racism, anti-racism and multiculturalism must be "deconstructed" and more fully theorized to provide clear psychological schemas within which new clinical paradigms and research methods can be formulated. [p. 23]

In the past decade, transcultural work has gained greater status and respect. It is especially important that an international group of professionals are now involved in exchanging ideas on theory, research, and the clinical process. The numbers of cross-cultural texts and research projects have multiplied at an amazing pace, reflecting the need for more discussion and challenges of these values. I still would like us to hold on to the fact that there is no "orthodox" way of working, and our tools are bringing an openness to relate with and understand the other within their individual and family psycho-social history and context.

Therapists such as Altman (1995) have shown great commitment to BME populations. He has challenged traditional views and
shown that it is quite a different process to work in the inner city
than to be in an affluent private consulting room. Speaking from a
relational perspective, he says, "psychoanalysis can no more be a
'blank screen' with respect to the impact of the social order on individual subjectivity than the analyst can be a 'blank screen' by virtue
of his silence" (1995, p. 75). Similarly, Adams adds: "I do not believe
that psychoanalysis can, by itself, realize the promise of multi-
culturalism, but I do believe that it has a valuable, potentially
unique contribution to make to the endeavour" (1996, p. xx). It is
fascinating that many of the recent texts are written by professionals (see Berzoff, Flanagan, & Hertz, 2002; Mishne, 2002) whose first
trainings were in the fields of social work and who later came to
train in the more "intrapsychic therapeutic arena".

The overall emphasis, throughout the book, is the significance of
the therapist's attitude and his/her underlying philosophical
stance. In therapy, it becomes essential to really allow room for the
client's material to be understood in the context of their psycho-
racial/cultural identity. We have to balance the inner, private self of
the client emerging within the cultural and racial context, but not
favouring one or the other. On this issue of cross-cultural issues,
Andreou (1999) writes that

> There are serious hazards in overestimating or ignoring them. To
> ignore them is to avoid a large part of the patient's and the thera-
> pist's everyday reality. To be over interested in them can represent
> an effort to deny and negate other deeper intrapsychic conflict.
> [1999, p. 76]

We must not get complacent, and make sure that our clients'
(conscious and unconscious) experiences have really been understood. This implies checking through verbal and non-verbal feedback and the general emotional atmosphere in the consulting room.
If our clients feel safe, and that their culture is validated, they will
share meaningful cultural elements. Otherwise, if they sense the
therapist's discomfort or unfamiliarity with the issues, they may
bring more neutral and impersonal cultural information, leaving
out the affect. This creates a distancing effect with the therapist, and

conveys such messages as "you do not understand my culture" and "you are not one of us", or "you do not know the culture", and, therefore, the meaningful elements will be kept at bay. The therapist has to be able to remain open-minded, and address whatever feelings arise. If a client feels comfortable enough with the therapist, then they will be able to step back from their culture far enough to be able to make a critique, be it positive or negative. The therapist's role is to remain open during such delicate exploration, and this can only be achieved through research and reading, and, above all, extensive personal development, rigorous professional and self analysis and reflection after therapy sessions, supervision, and peer discussions. I agree with Steiner (1996), who says,

> theory may in fact obstruct the analyst's capacity to open himself to the patient's material. Perhaps such disappointment with theory is a healthy state of affairs and leaves us aware that a good theory is a fine servant but a poor master. [p. 1082]

Cross-cultural therapy is often perceived as "marginal", and yet any encounter, even "white British" with "white British", can be viewed in terms of containing similarities and differences. Each party brings their own sub-culture, and there will be common ground as well as significant value differences. Psychotherapy cannot change stereotypes, but they can be challenged and understood on a micro-scale. We have to exercise flexibility and openness in our clinical work. I genuinely believe that cross-cultural therapy has a significant role to play in supporting individuals to engage more with their external cultural environment. This belief is supported not only by my clinical experiences (Eleftheriadou, 1994), but also by some fascinating neuro-imaging work, which has shown that the same brain areas are activated when there is social exclusion and rejection of one's group as when there is physical pain (Eisenberger, Lieberman, & Williams, 2003). More specifically, it was found that the anterior cingulated cortex (ACC) was more active during exclusion than during inclusion.

In conclusion, around the world, there is an increasing recognition that we are immersed in cultural (among many other) differences, especially those of us who choose to move, live, and work across cultural environments. It follows that in such an intimate enterprise as psychotherapy, we need to broaden our ways of thinking and working. A good (and creative) architect would never dream of constructing a building without taking into account the external environment, including the existing surrounding structure, even how weather conditions are likely to affect the structure and style of living. In the same way, we have kept culture as an outsider to therapy. If we address the fear of the unknown and understand what it is we do not know, or even what we think we do not know, we might find ourselves more comfortable with differences with our clients. Furthermore, there is no doubt that we also have to accept our limitations in working with racial and cultural issues; we cannot possibly know about all practices, or even accept all of them. Sometimes, it also means the client is ready to stop the work or be referred elsewhere. There are no easy answers to these clinical dilemmas, but we have to constantly consider them with other professionals and challenge ourselves. I would like to end with Pedersen, who is considered one of the "grandfathers" of cross-cultural psychology and counselling in the USA, who states, "During the past 20 years, multiculturalism has become recognized as a powerful force not just for understanding 'specific' groups but for understanding ourselves and those with whom we work" (1997, p. 4).

References

Adams, M. V. (1996). *The Multicultural Imagination: "Race", Color, and the Unconscious*. London: Routledge.

Altman, N. (1995). *The Analyst in the Inner City: Race, Culture, and Class through a Psychoanalytic Lens*. Hillsdale, NJ: Analytic Press.

Andreou, C. (1999). Some intercultural issues in the therapeutic process. In: M. Lanyado & A. Horne (Eds.), *Child and Adolescent Psychotherapy* (pp. 73–79). London: Routledge.

Berzoff, J., Flanagan, L. M., & Hertz, P. (Eds.). (2002). *Inside Out and Outside In: Psychodynamic Clinical Theory and Practice in Contemporary Multicultural Contexts*. Oxford, NJ: Jason Aronson.

Bhugra, D., & Bhui, K. (2006). Psychotherapy across the culture divide. In: R. Moodley & S. Palmer (Eds.), *Race, Culture and Psychotherapy* (pp. 46–57). London: Routledge.

Dalal, F. (2006). Culturalism in multicultural psychotherapy. In: R. Moodley & S. Palmer (Eds.), *Race, Culture and Psychotherapy* (pp. 36–45). London: Routledge.

Eisenberger, N. I., Lieberman, M. D., & Williams, K. D. (2003). Does rejection hurt? An fMRI study of social exclusion, *Science, 302*(5643): 290–292.

Eleftheriadou, Z. (1994). *Transcultural Counselling*. London: Central Books.

Fernando, S. (Ed.) (1995). *Mental Health in a Multi-Ethnic Society*. London: Routledge.

Fernando, S., & Keating, F. (2008). *Mental Health in a Multi-Ethnic Society* (2nd edn). London: Routledge.

Fernando, S., Ndegwa, D., & Wilson, M. (Eds.) (1998). *Forensic Psychiatry: Race and Culture*. London: Routledge.

Freud, S. (1918a). The Taboo of Virginity. *S.E.., 11*: 191–208. London: Hogarth.

Hawkes, B. (1999). Are black and ethnic minorities on trial? Thinking, psychoanalytically about family court work: a forensic and intercultural approach. *Psychodynamic Practice, 5*(2): 205–218.

Laungani, P. (2002). Understanding mental illness across cultures. In: S. Palmer (Ed.), *Multicultural Counselling: A Reader* (pp. 129–156). London: Sage.

Littlewood, R., & Lipsedge, M. (1989). *Aliens and Alienists*. London: Routledge.

Mishne, J. (2002). *Multiculturalism and the Therapeutic Process*. London: Guilford Press.

Moodley, R., & Palmer, S. (2006). Culture, race and other multiple constructions: an absent presence in psychotherapy. In: R. Moodley & S. Palmer (Eds.), *Race, Culture and Psychotherapy* (pp. 11–26). London: Routledge.

National Institute for Mental Health in England (NIMHE) (2003). *Real Voices: Survey Findings from a Series of Community Consultation Events Involving Black and Minority Ethnic Communities in England*. London: Department of Health.

Pedersen, P. (1997). *Culture-Centered Counseling Interventions*. Thousand Oaks, CA: Sage.

Steiner, J. (1996). The aim of psychoanalysis in theory and its practice. *International Journal of Psychoanalysis, 77*: 1073–1083.

CHAPTER TWO

Culture, race, and identity: meanings and complexities

Zack Eleftheriadou

T he aim of this chapter is to examine in depth the meanings of culture, race, and racism, and to emphasize how multi-faceted they are. There will be discussion of how human beings have a tendency to stereotype, or behave in a prejudiced manner, and how, as a result, we rigidly apply the concepts of race and culture, perceiving others as belonging to specific criteria. The emphasis here is to explore socialization as interplay between individual, familial, and cultural factors.

The cultural milieu

A good starting point is to consider what are all the "constructs" which constitute culture and how we can identify them. Culture is such a complex concept (Eleftheriadou, 1996), which has a profound influence on us, and yet its influence can be so subtle. It can be described as altering our lives intravenously, just like the air we breathe. The experience of living in one specific milieu places us in a particular "atmosphere", with which we become intertwined. It is a profound experience, and one that is often difficult to convey to others. This is because *we live culture*. Describing the true meaning of culture is not an easy process, as we are deeply emotionally involved with it. We absorb it in a way that we do not even realize it has filtered in. The word "culture" encompasses our *total* way of life.

In attempts to understand culture, we are not looking for a causation link, as if we can have straight, predictable links if we can know a "culture" or "cultural boundaries/beliefs" of a defined group or an individual. In fact, this often fails us in research studies, because it limits the complexity of human experience and reduces cultural factors. The aim is to identify that which is always present, influencing, but not necessarily in the most concrete, evident way. It is also not the aim, like social anthropologists, to identify universals. Generally, cultural experience does not have to be explained away (that is, in a reductionist approach) and may not even become an issue, unless one changes environment and has to convey to someone else what that experience was like, or, similarly, in a therapeutic relationship, where the two do not share the context. The psychodynamics are similar to the infant processing its experience with its primary care-giver. The subtle mother–infant interactions register, but they are so complex that even when we watch these interactions in slow motion, it can take some time to unravel and it certainly does not represent the whole picture.

Lago and Thomson's model (1996) of culture, using the "iceberg analogy", is useful, as they remind us of how many cultural influences are not visible, but are rather complex to describe. Culture includes observable behaviours, such as appearance and clothing. Cultural systems are important, but also we must guard that they do not become euphemisms for making generalizations that serve only to reinforce stereotypes. Furthermore, everything is embedded in a particular time frame and context. Culture is

> not a rigid or closed system of ideas. It is a flexible construction of the world to which a certain group of people belong, which is geographically and historically specific. It changes with each generation, as well as with the influx of others or exposure to other cultural constructions. [Eleftheriadou, 1994, p. 2]

Cultural boundaries are not clearly marked, as if we know where one culture begins and the other ends; it is definitely not as clear as we would sometimes like to think. The boundaries of what constitutes culture are changeable through time. Culture may also be described as simply what is meaningful to a group. For example, cultural songs and rhythms can bring people together. As Storr (1992) states, music and singing provide the cultural group with a profoundly emotional experience. Physiologically the arousal levels are synchronized during the shared experience. Some social psychologists have made the distinction between social system and culture; that is, that individuals/groups may not behave in ways that are predictable, or in congruence to their culture (Smith & Bond, 1998). For example, cultural events (like Christmas or Ramadan) may be celebrated by groups to achieve social networking, although it is not necessarily part of their belief/religious system.

Both the culture and the self are present at any one time, and when you are working with someone in the consulting room, there is always their culture in the background and you need to keep examining both at the same time. This is an interesting state to be in; at times, we dip in and out of cross-cultural differences, they can be in the background and then, at other times of one's life or therapy, they become poignant. This is the very dynamic we encounter *throughout* the cross-cultural therapeutic process.

There are the supportive aspects of a community or extended family; for example, one of my clients, Joshua, who tragically lost his partner, found going to synagogue, prayers and the support of members of his community extremely helpful in getting him through the initial shock and enabling him to start grieving. For this client, the cultural structure of what was to take place each night after the funeral helped him, as he found it unbearable to be alone at first. However, the cultural structure may not provide support to everyone. When describing culture, it tends to be politically correct to outline its positive aspects, but it is equally important to outline the negative aspects of culture, and, interestingly, there is slowly more of this writing through the eyes of minorities themselves. According to Dalal,

> All cultural systems (amongst other things) are the institutionalization of systems of oppression. If this is the case then one can no longer respect cultural difference in any straight-forward way, because the respect for cultural difference is inevitably to endorse,

and collude with, a system of oppression . . . it is no coincidence that it is usually those who are the beneficiaries of a cultural organization who tend to be its loudest defenders. [2006, p. 41]

Dalal goes on to say that: "cultures are structures, consisting of systems of power relations in which the rules are such that some of the groupings within that culture fare better than other groupings" (*ibid.*). Sadly, it is still the case that in most cultures women are worse off than men, but often the rationale of these cultural structures is not even questioned and is deeply ingrained. To this day, there are dramatic differences between sexes. A rare female account of the "traditional Arab position" is Ghada Kharmi's account (in which she writes very movingly of her experience of moving to Syria from Jerusalem), where she describes:

> Sons are prized over daughters and women were reared to indulge and look up to the males of the family. In return, males were expected to protect and support their mothers and sisters. But at the age of eight, this did not cut much ice with me. It just seemed an arrant injustice and I resented and hated my brother for it, as if it has been his fault. [2002, p. 134]

Similarly, in India, for example, sons are preferred because they are a way of obtaining economic security, especially when the parents reach old age and cannot work any more. There tends to be greater value placed on having many children, especially sons, therefore, and they are treated differently from girls and expected to be loyal to the family. Girls, on the other hand, are encouraged to create their own family and take care of their husband's household.

There are undoubtedly different evaluations of what is socially acceptable or not, depending on different interpretations. For example, it is not just the family that can induce guilt in a person, but rules and codes are imposed by one's (influential) cultural group and cultural socialization. Once again, Kharmi provides a moving account to illustrate this: one day she finds herself in the market area in Damascus and, because her head is not covered, she is grabbed by a man, who shouts at her that she is a "shameless girl" and blames her parents for having "no shame" (2002, p. 139). She is not only publicly shamed, but the parents are blamed. This is one example where the more collectivist type of society there is, the more blame is put on the family for an individual's behaviour than in a more individualistic structure. In this context, the (religious) stranger has more of a "right" (although it is arguable as to who has such a "right", but makes the point that personal freedom has different meanings in different socio-political contexts, especially where gender issues are concerned) to speak to her in this way than she was used to while living in Jerusalem (or what would be thought to be appropriate in a western country). However, it is essential to emphasize that it shows how even the interpretation of Islamic codes of dress differ according to the context. As a Palestinian girl, at that particular time, she was not used to covering her head in Jerusalem, so this experience came as quite a shock. In therapeutic work, one could not but look at issues of public shame, private guilt, and the influences of elders (even strangers) over the younger generation. The person would carry a greater sense of the community, and what one ought to be like and how one should dress/behave. Similarly, Watanabe talks about how "the mother needs her child to be good in the eyes of the public to save her face and prove her competence" (1992, p. 28). These codes of conduct are difficult to shed, particularly when one is immersed in a particular context. Sometimes, the only way to achieve this is to move contexts.

Socialization across cultures

Human development varies according to the cultural context (Kagitcibasi, 1996). De Zulueta suggests that from the very beginning

> The mother–infant relationship is itself embedded within a complex socio-biological matrix with which it interacts; it is a subsystem of the family system which itself is part of a larger social system and this has direct implications for how both mother and infant interact. [1993, p. 203]

"Enculturation" is the name given to the process of socialization through one's own culture. There may be specific didactic learning or learning by imitation, but there are clear expectations of learning the language and rituals, among many others. Culturally, there are expectations that there is "enough" transmission, but not necessarily the replication of behaviour. Enculturation can be broken down into other, different types of socialization, and each type will have a distinct impact. For example, the impact from the parents, or what has been called "vertical socialization", is usually the greatest in the earlier years in most cultures. In some cultures, this continues throughout the life span, with elders being respected and not disobeyed.

"Horizontal socialization" is used to describe the impact from peers; in some cultures, the impact may be greater from the same sex children, because in those cultures there is more segregation of their daily play or helping with chores. In western countries, such as the UK and the USA, children are encouraged to bond with peers by going on school trips. In more southern European cultures, children are accompanied by their parents on more family-centred outings where children follow the family friendships and relations more than individual peers. Also, in some southern European cultures, such as Greece and Cyprus, more people are defined as "relations". For example, the word "cousin" is generally used to refer to children of the parents' siblings, but also children of aunts and uncles. In the UK, we use the terms "second cousin", or "third cousin removed", which implies somewhat greater distance. Diagonal socialization consists of uncles, aunts, and grandparents who have an impact on the child's development. In some cultures, such as those of Mediterranean countries, the role of the grandparents or uncles/aunts is not only important, but essential in the child's upbringing. In other northern European societies, aunts and uncles may be grouped under "extended" family, and there is generally less influence by them. Similarly, gender differences are inevitably part of the important equation. Interestingly, gender differences seem to be greater in socio-economically less developed countries than in developed countries. The differences between genders still predominate universally, but with a significant decrease in countries where educational opportunities are greater.

Each country also has different norms regarding what is considered an appropriate life stage for certain things: for example, there is prescribed age and context for where a sexual relationship can begin, or the appropriate age for marriage, or becoming a parent (for instance, in western countries there are many older couples becoming parents). In some cultures, marriage is the prerequisite for the establishment of "independent" adulthood, while in other cultures it is encouraged that one lives alone first, or travels in order to gain different experiences before one marries. In other countries, this is not only discouraged, but tightly controlled.

Sense of "self" defined across cultures: individualism and collectivism

Psychologists (such as Triandis, 1988; Triandis, Bontempo, Villareal, Asai, & Lucca, 1988) have divided cultures into two types: individualistic and collectivist (see Table 1 for a brief overview of differences).

This distinction is a useful way of highlighting differences when the two ends of the spectrum are studied: for example, those countries that may favour independence and those that promote a group

Table 1. An overview of differences between individualistic and collectivist cultures.

Individualistic (e.g. USA and UK)	Collectivist (e.g. South European, South American, and East Asian cultures
Focus on self-goals	Subordination to the family
Focus on personal wishes and needs	Subordination to the collective
Less influence from the group	Boundaries are discouraged and seen as an obstacle
Autonomy is encouraged	Autonomy is viewed negatively (Kakar, 1981)
Individualistic needs and goals are more important	Collectivist needs and goals are more important, especially in societies like like Japan
	In some countries, there is greater control in terms of art, religion, politics, science, etc.

(*continued*)

Table 1.   (*continued*)

Individualistic (e.g. USA and UK)	Collectivist (e.g. South European, South American, and East Asian cultures
Less collectivism on a national scale	Collectivism on a national scale is encouraged More rigid groups
Individual competition	More hierarchical system, according to sex, age and status
Linear time and youth emphasis on what the person does	Emphasis on who the people are Interest in background, especially religious or political affiliations
Interest is slight for person's background	Direct experience from the elderly groups is considered important.
Written tradition	
The more complex and industrialized a society, the more busy it is, and the more attention is paid to time; e.g., Sweden and Japan	Sense of time is different
More specific roles People may only relate for a specific reason at a specific setting; fewer personal details necessary	Diffusion and greater overlap of roles More personal details required and considered appropriate
"In-groups" are less exclusive, more detached, flexible groups	"In-groups" are more exclusive, less trusting of strangers, conflicts are solved within the group
Members are usually more intimate with several groups simultaneously	High value on family background and status
Less concern about public criticism and reputation More individualistic type of guilt	Public criticism, judgement and reputation: for example, Arab cultures Guilt and shame notions
"Looser" cultures Less homogeneity	"Tighter" cultures
Less predictability, certainty, and security	More predictability

identity and belongingness. Individualism has implicit ideas on respecting people's physical and psychological "space". However, the research outcomes can only provide a distilled version of the myriad and complex behaviours and values. In most countries, there are both individualistic ways and collectivist ways of being, and they vary in degrees. For example, in Arab countries and some Mediterranean countries, it would be common that children live in close proximity to their parents after they move out of the family home (see the case of Leila, Eleftheriadou, 1997b). This could be described as a more collectivist characteristic. However, they would be encouraged to do certain things independently from a young age.

According to Smith and Bond, "in collectivist cultures, role and context will provide a greater share of the necessary cues" (1998, p. 78). Laungani gives an interesting cultural example:

> The death of an elderly person in a Hindu family is not just a private family affair. It affects the family's immediate relatives (the baradari), their sub-caste (jati) and the local community of which the deceased was a part. Anyone who knew the deceased in any significant capacity is obliged to come to the funeral. Not to come to the funeral is social transgression. In contradistinction to a Hindu funeral, a typical middle-class Anglican funeral is often seen as a private family's affair. Only those specifically invited may attend the funeral. [1999, p. 42]

Unravelling the concept of "race"

Race is a biologically invalid concept and has no scientific basis, but it has taken time for this incorrect notion to be challenged. And yet, sadly, people are categorized in terms of race far too readily (I urge the reader to look closely at newspaper headlines, even just over one single week). Unfortunately, "race" is often linked purely to colour and often used as "denial of similarity" (Dalal, 2006). Colour does not convey any information about a person's way of thinking, behaviour, relating, etc. According to Fernando (1991), race constitutes of all the observable differences between people. Often, people's behaviours are attributed to their race, and considered, therefore, to be unchangeable, like skin colour. At times, different concepts have been used to replace "race", which have been equally denigratory. For example, "culturalism" has been used to imply that when there are social problems, they have been attributed to people's different colours (Dalal, 2006). Additionally, socio-biological differences can be emphasized to such a degree that they take us back to a concrete boundary, excluding the notion that people have a race, but also a private, inner world.

Race has a particular meaning in a particular context; race itself is a more ambiguous concept and less concrete than many would like to think. The meaning of race is individual, but it is learnt in a cultural context. In a way, it may be more appropriate to talk about racism, which is real and active, than about "race". It is often difficult to pin down as racism, and often takes place indirectly. However, it has a powerful dehumanizing element and can be conscious or unconscious. Using the ideas of Franz Fanon (1991) (the Martinique psychoanalyst and writer who had a profound influence on the issues of decolonization) for a "new humanism", Walcott suggests "the history of racialisation and domination continue to impact on contemporary conditions" (2006, p. 29), once again emphasizing how the black category has been taken out of being human. Furthermore, we can argue that there is no black without white, and vice versa; they remain as the two co-existing polarities that require each other for discourse.

In therapeutic work, it is particularly of interest to realize how issues of race and culture may remain unconscious, as they are too difficult or painful to be thought about. The process of "projection" comes into play, where the notion of race is projected or placed into the other, who is seen as "different", and those differences are considered to be simply unbridgeable. Of course, the true racist is just as damaged as the people they project their feelings into. At the same time, this argument does not suggest that we are all the same, or that we should strive to be the same, but that there can be engagement with differences.

Many ethnic minority groups experience social deprivation in terms of housing, education, employment, and health care. Because of these external factors, racism is often seen as an external or socio-political issue, but, of course, it filters into the psychological.

Racism is

> everyone's concern because it is linked with human deprivation, a
> hierarchical system, lack of human freedom and dignity. Racism

creates feelings of envy, anger, jealousy, aggression, greed, deprivation, mistrust, fear and powerlessness and it is vital that is
worked with on an inter-psychic and intra-psychic level.
[Eleftheriadou, 1999, p. 119]

Inevitably, racism remains a very emotive and complicated issue
and has many components. Ridley (1995) differentiates between the
disposition to something, in other words, "prejudice", and the
observable behaviours, or what is labelled "racism". He believes
that one does not necessarily lead to the other. In order to understand racism, we need to tackle both levels, as people's beliefs do
not necessarily tally with how they behave. Throughout the book,
many questions are raised about the impact of racism on a micro-
scale (referring to the therapeutic consulting room) and the links
with macro-scale issues (referring to larger scale racism which
exists in groups and organizations). It is common that the shift of
blame in organizations can go to those who hold less power and are
more vulnerable, or what has been called "organizational racism"
(Palmer & Laungani, 1999; Ridley, 1995; also see Chapter Twelve in
this text).

As Tuckwell states,

While overt racist behaviour and discriminatory practices have
increasingly been vetoed by successive acts of legislation in the UK
and elsewhere, the legacy of white supremacy and black sub-
servience continues to be played out in many covert ways in
society, thus perpetuating existing power differentials. [2006,
p. 139]

Psycho-cultural/racial identity

This section will introduce the whole process of how cultural and
racial elements are incorporated to form a person's psycho-social
identity (except mixed race identity, which is discussed in Chapter
Seven). As the subject of identity is vast, the focus here will be on
these racial and cultural elements rather than parental influences,
although in later chapters these are addressed more, particularly
through the case material. Psycho-cultural and racial influences on
identity are a running thread throughout the book.

Some theorists have focused on the concept of "race" to define identity, but a broader view of psycho-cultural and psycho-racial factors will be examined in this context. Erikson (1987), a psycho-analyst who worked closely with anthropologists studying, among many others, the Sioux and Yurok Indians in South Dakota in the USA, believed that the psyche is embedded in the social. He suggested that personal identity is a continual developmental process with the influence of social and cultural forces. He believed that from early life a child is influenced by the care-giver, who, in turn, is influenced by their own socialization (see Holmes, 1995). It is hardly surprising that he held these views, since he himself was part of a mixed parentage and step-parentage, and as a family they travelled a great deal, so that he was constantly aware of issues of identity. He emphasized the impact of history, geography, and culture on different ways of living and child rearing, all of which are normal within their particular societies. Similarly, Kakar, a psychoanalyst influenced by Erikson, examines cross-cultural work in the context of Indian culture. He states,

> Identity . . . is meant to convey the process of synthesis between inner life and outer social reality as well as the feeling of personal continuity and consistency within oneself. It refers to the sense of having a stake in oneself, and at the same time in some kind of confirming community. Identity has other connotations, perspectives which extend beyond the individual and the social to include the historical and the cultural. [1981, p. 2]

Identity is a complicated construct, consisting of many elements; there is a developmental strand (parental psycho-social influences and identifications), individual preferences, and cultural similarities and expectations, as shown below:

Summary of psycho-cultural and racial identity influences

Cultural beliefs and values and how they define expectations

What is the client's "culture" and is this, or how is it, different to their birth country culture? How would their culture be described to someone from the same origin and someone of another culture?

What are the different dynamics? What are other sub-cultures they belong to? Where have those influences come from?

- Paternal/maternal/others' roots of migration (including adjustment patterns, relationships with those from the same/ other cultural/racial groups)?
- Definition of appropriate behaviour/limits (if any) on "acceptable" behaviour.
- Authority and decision making in the family: are there formal kinship patterns?
- Behaviours, rituals, support systems linked to the cultural group.
- Emotional meanings attached to historic, religious, spiritual places of worship.
- The surrounding landscape and layout, architectural buildings.
- The climate/weather: impact of the self and body within a particular landscape.

The family

Enculturation influences, vertical and horizontal socialization.

- What are the family beliefs, appropriate behaviours, family cycle tasks, life stages?
- Does the family use "traditional" values (learnt from the family, such as from grandparents, for example).
- Which values are currently used or have these traditional ideas been lost/rejected?
- What are the particular stressors/losses for that individual, their family (how explicit are these to the person; some may remain unconscious or are just never [allowed to be] discussed in the family).
- How is the family organized; for example, how are the gender roles organized?
- What is the neighbourhood or immediate environment of the family? Does this support or split family (cultural/racial/ ethnic) identity? Does it scatter them or bring the family closer together?

Language

● What languages are spoken and at what level?
● Which one is the fluent one?
● What language does the client associate with their emotional life and which is one with their social life?
● What language is associated with important life stages?
● What are other significant words used to describe their culture?

Individual and cultural identity (in both the old and new society)

● Internal role: how one experiences him/herself.
● Intrapersonal: how one experiences relating to others.
● External role: how the new/old society views the person and their experiences (for example, have these been welcoming or rejecting?).

Adjustment

What is the overall experience within the host culture?

● Functional: that is, have they "adjusted" only in order to survive in the new culture?
● Cognitive: do they understand the way of thinking in the new culture?
● Emotional: is there involvement in the new culture's values?

    Continuity/discontinuity of culture.

● If any, what is the nature of contact with those left behind?
● Have other relatives/children/grandchildren also emigrated?
● Peers from the same culture who have also emigrated.

What constitutes identity also depends on what is imposed by the context, and therefore might be defined in a wide or narrow way; for example, most of my Afro-Caribbean colleagues have learnt the wide label "black" in the UK, but back at "home" this might not have been used at all, and they identified themselves with a narrower label, although strong island identity, such as being a Trinidadian, or a Jamaican. It is clear that no one is "culturally pure" (either historically or in terms of the increasing trends of mixed cross-cultural/racial parentage). Identity and belongingness is rather complex, as an individual may belong to one culture and their family may identify with another. We also know from other social psychology work that we all hold different identities as individuals and can behave in contrary ways when in a group setting. But the crucial question to raise here is: how does a culture or community group or family influence one's racial, cultural, political (among many) affiliations chosen? Nowadays, the theoretical thinking of identity formation seems to have shifted more towards the notion of "multiple identity", or multiple selves. A vivid description of this comes from Meri Nana-Ama Danueq, a black American woman who wrote about her depression and journey to recovery. She describes herself as: "I am black; I am female; I am an immigrant. Every one of these labels plays an equally significant part in my perception of myself and the world around me" (1999, pp. 224–225). Of course, at different times, there can be overlap between the different aspects of identity as well as conflict.

There is also a fluid identity, which is multi-dimensional and complex. Thomas and Schwarzbaum state that

> Individuals need to integrate their particular traits, their ideal self, and perceptions of others, including current perceptions and historical stereotypical roles, as they form their self-perceptions across the life span. Therefore, the sense of self is not developed in a vacuum, but within multiple contexts. [2005, p. 4]

There is also the question of whether these multiple selves are present or past influences. Moodley and Palmer shed light on this by highlighting how

> Individuals are often torn between the need to experience themselves existentially in the "here and now", and the desire to be historically or psychically connected to a specific, but not too distant, past. This may be constructed in ethnic, cultural and racial terms. In essence the subjective "self" manages both the inner psychological world and outer social, cultural and political environments. [2006, p. 19]

For black people, there is a collective memory of slavery and colonization (as discussed further in Chapters Two and Eleven) and for white people, dominance and privilege. Inevitably, these historical and social experiences have a tremendous and cumulative influence on intrapsychic development. Although dramatic changes have been seen globally, it is still not uncommon to find that white people are in a position of power and authority and black people are being pushed down the social hierarchy and experiencing ongoing racism. This takes place on both conscious and unconscious levels and results in internalized beliefs regarding inferiority that are hard to penetrate and change.

Identity formation begins from infancy in the most profound and subtle ways. Just as there may be a sense of identification with one parent and not the other at different developmental stages, there may have to be a degree of "splitting" (or viewing one culture as positive and the other as negative) at times, in order to obtain an optimal or positive self-identity.

The existential and phenomenological schools of thought (Spinelli, 1989; van Deurzen-Smith, 1988) have described identity in terms of a "worldview" to encompass the different aspects of a person's experience and weave together the inner and outer worlds. Therefore, the concept worldview consists of the *uberwelt*, or spiritual world (which may be spiritual beliefs or, more traditionally, religious beliefs), the *umwelt*, or the physical world (how a person feels, being in their physical world), the *mitwelt*, or social world (includes any significant groups a person may belong to), and all of these form the *eigenwelt*, or the most intimate sense of the person (see Eleftheriadou, 1997b, 2002, for more detail).

In previous writings (Eleftheriadou, 1997a), I have represented the relationship of self and culture as a spring that represents the link between the self and the culture or a person's worldview. The spring can stretch for some people (as shown by the case examples in later chapters), for example, those who are forced to move, or choose to move further away from their cultural heritage, or can be very closely linked for others. The latter refers to those that perhaps choose a more "communal way" (see individualistic/collectivist discussion as discussed earlier in this chapter) of being, or that is all they have been exposed to and it has never been questioned. It does imply, though, that the spring is not static; it has movement, so the relationship of self and culture is continually changing (as discussed in this chapter). In psychotherapy, it is useful to find out about all these influences in the person's life and assessment issues, or the person's psycho-racial/cultural identity. How this unfolds is just as interesting as its content. For example, there may be a client who behaves as if there is no link with their cultural roots, they have an Anglicized name attached to a foreign surname, and it feels as if the spring has been cut. Another person may hold on to it as a façade and keep others, including the therapist, at a distance. Of course, it does not mean that we make cross-cultural issues become an issue, if the person seems at ease with them. However, in an intimate or therapeutic relationship, one would expect to have some conversation about the clients' roots, and if there is lack of information it might alert us to losses, dislocation, confusion, or their struggle to separate; therefore, historical information is kept at bay.

In conclusion, this chapter has demonstrated that there is a huge variation between cultures and sub-cultures. Unravelling these concepts informs clinical practice and, one hopes, broadens our perception of our clients and their experiences. We need to challenge ourselves about holding a set view of the "self", which has not only been predominant in psychology, but has also been the central issue of western psychotherapy and counselling.

As discussed earlier, "culture" does do not simply shape us, but the impact is complex and deep. It appears that there are different ways of behaving which are culturally adaptable. As stated earlier, racial and cultural messages and labels of other groups are learnt by children automatically, with little if any questioning. However, it is always an interesting exercise to pause and consider when societal influences might creep in and how much evidence we really have for the individual/familial views we hold. We often make gross generalizations (which we hold on to rigidly) without substantial information to back them up.

The concept of race determines many of the social rules and norms and can be described as the most visible difference. None the less, the race-based approach is not promoted in this book, as race/ skin colour is seen as *only one* of the countless characteristics of one's identity. The numerous components mentioned in this chapter provide the "stepping stone" for later chapters, which address how racial and cultural factors shape the individual's identity or ethnicity and how they are taken into consideration in transcultural psychotherapy. It is important to resist too many labels around race, as most people (in clinical and non-clinical settings) would not define themselves in such a narrow way and, similarly to the discussion around culture, meanings of race change over time (also see Chapters Six and Seven, which examine the fluidity of people's identities).

This chapter has emphasized that race and ethnicity are socially constructed (containing psychological factors and, of course, also an overlap on wider socio-political issues) and will inevitably have an impact on the therapeutic process and relationship. In the therapeutic arena, these will need to be thought about *together* with the client. The therapist has to have the psychological capacity to enter the other's inner landscape, or at least strive to understand the major components. The client will be filled with different ideas on societal racial hierarchy and constructions about the "racial other". There are many different scenarios as to how these unfold, which are explored through clinical material in later chapters. But whatever one's therapeutic approach,

> Counsellors cannot easily dismiss their responsibility in combating racism. Even counsellors who are not bigots participate in a larger system that victimizes minorities. Using ineffectual interventions, misdiagnosing clients, and imposing biased cultural expectations are among the many ways minorities are victimised in counselling. No client deserves this type of mistreatment. Certainly, mental health professionals face a great challenge. But if they do not at least try to stop racism, they actually behave in a racist manner by allowing it to continue. [Ridley, 1995, pp. 22–23]

The latter part of the chapter outlined the influences on people's psycho-racial/cultural identity. The overview can inform therapists of how racial and cultural experiences can affect one's capacity to be in a new environment and the ability to maintain old attachments or form new attachments with people of the same/different cultural backgrounds. People have different psycho-social resources/types of personality to manage this, which also determines how they mix with those from other cultures. We need to hold on to all the elements, sometimes literally fragments of their identity, in order to work towards some sense of identity integration. The list of influences acts as a checklist for the therapist rather than a prescriptive list to follow.

References

Dalal, F. (2006). Culturalism in multicultural psychotherapy. In: R. Moodley & S. Palmer (Eds.), *Race, Culture and Psychotherapy* (pp. 36–45). London: Routledge.

Danueq, M. N. A. (1988). *Willow Weep for Me: A Black Woman's Journey Through Depression*. New York: W. W. Norton, 1998.

De Zulueta, F. (1993). *From Pain to Violence: The Traumatic Roots of Destructiveness*. London: Whurr.

Eleftheriadou, Z. (1994). *Transcultural Counselling*. London: Central Books.

Eleftheriadou, Z. (1996). Notions of culture. In: S. Sharples (Ed.), *Changing Cultures: Developments in Cross-Cultural Theory and Practice* (pp. 7–13). London: UKCOSA.

Eleftheriadou, Z. (1997a). Cultural differences in the therapeutic process. In: I. Horton & V. Varma (Eds.), *The Needs of Counsellors and Psychotherapists* (pp. 68–83). London: Sage.

Eleftheriadou, Z. (1997b). The cross-cultural experience: integration or isolation. In: S. Du Plock (Ed.), *Case Studies in Existential Psychotherapy and Counselling* (pp. 59–69). Chichester: Wiley.

Eleftheriadou, Z. (1999). Assessing the counselling needs of ethnic minorities in Britain. In: P. Laungani & S. Palmer (Eds.), *Counselling in a Multi-cultural Society* (pp. 113–132). London: Sage.

Eleftheriadou, Z. (2002). Transcultural counselling and psychotherapy: a philosophical framework. In: S. Palmer (Ed.), *Multicultural Counselling* (pp. 31–39). London: Sage.

Erikson, E. H. (1987). *A Way of Looking at Things: Selected Papers*, S. Schlein (Ed.). London: Norton.

Fanon, F. (1991). *Black Skins, White Masks*. London: Pluto Press.

Fernando, S. (1991). *Race, Culture and Mental Health*. London: Macmillan/Mind.

Holmes, R. M. (1995). *How Young Children Perceive Race*. London: Sage.

Kagitcibasi, C. (1996). *Family and Human Development across Cultures*. Mahwah, NJ: Lawrence Erlbaum.

Kakar, S. (1981). *The Inner World*. Delhi: Oxford University Press.

Kharmi, G. (2002). *In Search of Fatima: A Palestinian Story*. London: Verso.

Laungani, P. (1999). Culture and identity: implications for counselling. In: S. Palmer & P. Laungani, P. (Eds.), *Counselling in a Multicultural Society* (pp. 35–70). London: Sage.

Moodley, R., & Palmer, S. (2006). *Race, Culture and Psychotherapy*. London: Routledge.

Palmer, S., & Laungani, P. (Eds.) (1999). *Counselling in a Multicultural Society*. London: Sage.

Ridley, C. R. (1995). *Overcoming Unintentional Racism in Counselling and Therapy*. London: Sage.

Smith, P. B., & Bond, M. H. (1998). *Social Psychology Across Cultures*. London: Prentice Hall.

Spinelli, E. (1989). *The Interpreted World: An Introduction to Phenomenological Psychology*. London: Sage.

Storr, A. (1992). *Music and the Mind*. London: HarperCollins.

Thomas, A. J., & Schwarzbaum, S. (2006). *Culture and Identity*. London: Sage.

Triandis, H. C. (1988). Collectivism vs. individualism: a reconceptualization of a basic concept in cross-cultural social psychology. In: C. Bagley & G. K. Verma (Eds.), *Personality, Cognition and Values* (pp. 60–95). London: Macmillan.

Triandis, H. C., Bontempo, R., Villareal, M. J., Asai, M., & Lucca, N. (1988). Individualism and collectivism: cross-cultural perspectives on self-group relationships. *Journal of Personality and Social Psychology*, *54*: 323–338.

Tuckwell, G. (2006). Psychodynamic counselling, "race" and culture. In: S. Wheeler (Ed.), *Difference and Diversity in Counselling* (pp. 137–155). New York: Palgrave.

Walcott, R. (2006). Multiculturally crazy: diagnosis in Black. In: R. Moodley & S. Palmer (Eds.), *Race, Culture and Psychotherapy* (pp. 27–35). London: Routledge.

Van Deurzen-Smith, E. (1988). *Existential Counselling in Practice*. London: Sage.

Watanabe, H. (1992). Difficulties in Amae: a clinical perspective. *Infant Mental Health Journal*, *1*(1): 26–33.

CHAPTER THREE

Pre-transference, transference, and countertransference

Zack Elefetheriadou

T his chapter will outline the psychoanalytic concepts of pre-transference, transference, and countertransference in detail. They are such significant aspects of the clinical work that they warrant a detailed explanation alongside case material before further aspects of the clinical relationship are outlined. Although some of the issues discussed in this chapter relate to working with refugees, they also have their own unique dynamics; hence, issues directly related to refugees are discussed in separate chapters (see Chapters Nine and Ten).

From the first session, the therapist takes into account the dynamics of transference and countertransference. Transference and countertransference are psychoanalytic concepts that are used to describe the feelings evoked between the client and the therapist. Freud (1895d) was the first to talk about the concept of transference when he outlined his observations on how (as they were then described) "hysterical patients" were falling in love with their physicians. At first, he wrote about this as a hindrance, but he later realized that this could be useful in therapeutic work. Today, it is believed that this is part of every encounter, and clinically it is extremely informative about the client's emotional state and relationships. Transference includes the feelings a client holds for those who are most intimate to them (usually stemming from childhood relationships with their primary care-givers) and how they were treated by them. These are projected to (or placed on to) the therapist. Similarly, countertransference refers to the way the therapist may also place, or, in psychoanalytic terms, project, their own feelings on to the client, or the way in which their own feelings can be triggered by a similar emotional experience to that of their client. These feelings can often be intensified when the therapist belongs to the same culture as the person or their care-givers (Akhtar, 2006). Countertransference is such a useful tool, even with clients who are not fluent in the English language. Acquarone says,

> Even when I could not verbally transmit my understanding of the situation, I would patiently allow myself to experience their spontaneous behaviour, comments, and expression of feelings, allowing my countertransference to guide me. This suggests to me how useful such nonverbal methods of communication can be for transmitting containments, acceptance, respect of customs, etc. [2004, p. 177]

Curry (1964) has extended the concept of transference to the concept of "pre-transference", or "societal transference". This incorporates all that the client may transfer from their societal experiences to the therapeutic relationship. After all, the consulting room is not a confined place that keeps external racial, cultural, and political dynamics out; in fact, they can be intensified, particularly at times of anxiety (Samuels, 1993): for example, how clients perceive their status within the majority culture. This notion refers to all the feelings that clients experience even before they have met the therapist. In the same way, the therapist will have their own views on what the client will be like. The transference is highly charged with racial and cultural history dynamics (Akhtar, 2006). Tuckwell says,

> Transference and countertransference as relating to blackness and whiteness are therefore associated with internalized attitudes of white superiority and black subservience, and these may be manifested in emotional reactions to fear, mistrust, anger, guilt, suspicion and compliance. [2006, p. 150]

Being a therapist from a minority background means you need to be well prepared for questions or comments from clients. These issues may emerge as purely unconscious material. However, this is not the experience of my white, mainstream colleagues, and maybe we need to think about where the "wondering" of their clients goes? What I am referring to is that all our clients wonder (some have stronger images of what they imagine) about our background, marital status, sexuality, about our colour and culture. among many other issues. Being a therapist who is not easily ethnically distinguishable by appearance and working in a multicultural city like London, I have had a plethora of client perceptions. I have been described by clients as "mixed culturally", "half this and half that", "politically black", "Greek and something", and often perceived as "mixed" or "mixed race" by mixed race young people. Some of the labels projected on to us may seem more comfortable than others, but we need to feel comfortable enough in the therapeutic space to be able to hold them in mind and explore what meaning they have for the client at that moment in time, and what they are communicating in relation to us.

Clients not only react to societal transference, but may also spend time introducing it in the therapy. One personal experience of this was with a young client, Ben. During one therapy session, Ben started shouting racial abuse at passers-by. In the context of the therapy, I understood this as his unconscious way of bringing the issues into the consulting room. It induced enormous sadness in me, and some sense of being very far away from him, which is perhaps what he was feeling, emotionally distant and misunderstood by his parents, peers, and his teachers. Of course, unconsciously, he wondered how I would react to this, and I had to carefully digest the material and help him make sense of it (see Eleftheriadou, 2006, for further discussion). When the material comes in with such force, it may be a way of seeing or testing the therapist and a way of introducing racial/cultural issues before the therapist does. If this dynamic can be acknowledged and discussed, it can help the person address other significant parts of their emotional experience that they may wish to explore. In this case, Ben was wondering about whether my colleagues were my friends. Since, in this particular setting, my colleagues were evidently from different cultural and racial backgrounds, I thought he was wondering how I relate to people of different cultures, but, of course, how he and I would relate, since we were from different racial/cultural backgrounds. This opened up issues of having to negotiate a therapeutic relationship with someone who has had such negative cross-cultural and racial experiences. He needed to know about how much exposure I had had to different cultural viewpoints and whether I would allow room for the differences between us. The societal labels can not only be a hindrance to emotional exploration, but they also fragment the person by perceiving them only as a race or labels. As Mukherjee writes of the many labels directed on to different ethnic communities in the USA,

> We are expatriates, exiles, slaves and dispossessed, we are conquerors, plunderers, refugees, and amnesty-seekers, we are temporary workers, undocumented workers, visitors, students, tourists, we are joy-seekers, claim jumpers, parole-violators. [1999, p. 85]

Another clinical example is of a mixed race client who had a Greek Cypriot mother and an African father, who talked to me about how she knew immediately that I was Greek and often thought "I looked at her in the same way as her mother". For this client, the mere fact that I was of the same cultural background as her mother evoked material that had not been considered before. She had never felt accepted by her mother or her (mother's) cultural group, and yet she found herself in a therapeutic relationship with someone who was accepting, despite the cultural differences. If I had not had a therapy vacancy, then I am not sure she would have chosen to work with anyone Greek. She often enquired about my cross-cultural involvements, but I would refrain from giving her the information. I strongly believe it is important to allow room for the client's imagination to flourish rather than feel obliged to respond to cultural questions because, as this example illustrates, transference and countertransference feelings are complicated further by issues of culture. The therapist needs to be able to judge whether an answer about the therapist's country of origin will help the client examine further material or whether it will interfere with the relationship at that particular moment. When our clients ask questions about us, we need to wonder why they need to know and why it has become important at that point in time.

Holmes (1992) states that there is some evidence that black (here black refers to African-American) therapists will experience less negative countertransference with black patients. Well trained black therapists may enable a black client to be more open regarding racial experiences, and they are not driven in the same way by stereotypical behaviour; of course, this also provides more opportunities for identification with the therapist.

A vivid account of how cultural, racial, and family influences are linked with psychiatric disorders is provided in Danueq's account of her experience as a black American woman suffering from depression. She goes on to describe her experience with her second therapist, who is white, saying,

> But if he was having a difficult time understanding the overt issues of my life—like racism—was there any way that he could be grasping the subtle ones? Racism is definitely in the eye of the beholder. White people have at hand the privilege of choosing whether to see or not see the racism that takes place around them. If Dr. Fitzgerald could not "fathom" my reality as a black person, how could he be able to assess or address the rage, the fear, and the host of the complex emotions that go hand-in-hand with being black in a racist society? For whatever reasons, seeing a black therapist had never crossed my mind, until then. [1999, p. 224]

She then goes on to say,

> I do not believe that white therapists are unable to successfully treat people of color; however, I do think that they should possess a certain level of cultural sensitivity, as that culture plays an important role in both the patient's illness and treatment. [ibid.]

Clearly, she gained a lot of support and insight into her life working with the white psychiatrist, Dr Fitzgerald. Even though he had not shared her racial or cultural experience, his honesty about his lack of experience of racism touched her. However, she still felt alone with the issues, and later talks about working with Shelly, a white Australian therapist, and how she felt "completely at ease" with her, as she was a foreigner herself. Furthermore, it was easier to talk with a female about her experience of sexual abuse. Interestingly, it was much later, when she worked with a black female psychiatrist, that she talked about working on her relationship with her mother and "making peace with her" (*ibid.*, p. 245). Clients who have never had the opportunity for this kind of self/race "mirroring" might find it useful to be matched to a racially similar therapist (who is suitably qualified and where the therapist and client match has been well thought out).

The term "mirroring" was originally coined by Winnicott to imply being seen in the eyes of the other. He states, "when I look I am seen, so I exist. I can now afford to look and see. I now look creatively and what I apperceive I also perceive" (1967, p. 114). (He means, through being seen by the other, one then sees him/herself, and then one is able to move to perception of, or differentiating between, a sense of what is me and not-me.) In this context, the concept of mirroring is used twofold: to refer to how much a client views the therapist as having the same part of themselves or expressing a part of themselves, or being different; there may be a sense of "we are the same", or that "we are so different". Both of these stem from psychological upbringing and how the individual has integrated their unconscious socialization experiences. The second way I am using mirroring is for the context, implying the way one looks at the other as representing their race and culture (or not, as the case might be). In other words, the way that the other culture is acknowledged. Cultural mirroring may be what they need, especially when there are negative social images of their country, or in the new country about their country of origin. This also opens up the whole issue of what it means to be a person of black racial origin who has had absent care-givers and poor self-esteem and standing in society to experience being in a trusting, close relationship with another black person.

Racial and cultural matching does not automatically imply that therapeutic trust will develop or be maintained. In fact, there is no guarantee whether the trust will develop, depending on their previous experiences from people of that cultural or racial group. The flip side of racial/cultural matching is that we also know that therapists can over-identify with the issues, and generally the whole social reality, and not leave sufficient room for the internal world to be expressed. Chin (1994) reminds us that if therapists are too sensitive, or over-identified with racial issues, then the client can be protected (or over-protected) from them and not challenged on more intrapsychic issues. This is an interesting issue to consider in terms of white therapists working with white clients also. Chin (1994) also believes there is also under-diagnosis of psychopathology with those of "colour" in the USA. Comas-Diaz and Jacobsen (1991) talk about fears of engulfment. Mishne (2002) also mentions that minority ethnic women in the USA show higher esteem for white authority figures and men of all backgrounds. In my professional experience, this dynamic also applies to the UK.

There are some common reactions when working with people of other cultures that any of us can get drawn into.

- We have got caught up with so much "political correctness" that it can often feel like a "straitjacket", rather than a respectful way of addressing and thinking about our differences.
- There can be a paralysis in that people often fear that they might offend, so they actually feel rather impotent.
- We can get into a "patronizing way" as if we have become the self-appointed spokesperson for minorities, which is extremely unhelpful.
- Therapists utilize an "individualizing" stance, where clients are seen as separate from their culture, or hold to the myth that colour does not matter (McGoldrick, 1998).

As Laird (1998) points out, it can become difficult to listen when one's own cultural texts are so powerful. If the client's story is so alien to the therapist's, there may be lack of empathic alliance. Clients from different backgrounds will evoke stereotypes, which we need to challenge along the way. However, this is difficult if there is no common ground and the therapist finds it hard to relate to the client. It is also not uncommon that the client is not completely involved with the cultural group that we initially perceived. So, the question remains as to how do we listen to our clients in a respectful, open, manner so that all the above-mentioned material can unfold? I think the more personal development we can undertake on these issues, the more refined our listening becomes towards our clients. It creates the paradox that the more we can be attuned to differences, the more liberated we can become to work with clients from cultural and racial backgrounds different to our own. Our own personal and cultural narratives have to be explored first before we make any attempt to explore those of the clients. As Liggan and Kay state: "It is not the race of the therapist but the acknowledgement of race that is crucial to the therapeutic interaction. Dynamic psychotherapy should recognize the influence of culture and ethnicity regarding the patient's emotional problems" (2006, p. 112).

There is a strong tradition within psychoanalysis and psychoanalytic psychotherapy to be suspicious and view the client's material as being about something else, something that has been significantly altered and deeply hidden. The client's material can fall under one of the following three categories: first, there may be reported material in the session, which, in fact, stands for something else and is yet out of the client's awareness. The client may attach the material to racial and cultural material, but the material is not necessarily about racial and cultural issues. For example, an angry client who felt belittled by their father may try to belittle ethnic minorities because it makes them feel superior. Second, their material may be conveying real external experiences that have taken place (of course, the person adds their personal interpretation and meanings to these real experiences' "factual details") and they need to be understood by the therapist as such. For example, the clients may hold experiences of prejudice (due to their accent, appearance, or name) that they experienced as an immigrant in the UK. Third, there can be a combination of both types of narrative.

Some clients come to therapy with the wish to explore their cultural milieu, and this process may entail some accepting, reviewing, and leaving behind some cultural patterns and ideas. Other clients will want to work specifically within their cultural setting. Each person makes it clear what is *negotiable* during the process of therapy. It is a complicated process to establish how much of a client's distress is linked to cultural issues and how much it is linked to more personal issues (which are still embedded in a cultural milieu, but culture is not the main focus). At any rate, clients seem to work best with someone who can take into account their cultural milieu and recognizes racism, so that the client does not feel it is only their personal problem.

The following vignettes illustrate the complex link between the client's experience of racism and how it becomes linked to her personal issues, as well as how it filters into the therapeutic relationship. These are cases where we are reminded that caution is necessary before giving feedback in relation to the client's racial and cultural material. The right interpretation at the wrong time may be devastating for our clients. If something is in the air and we share it with the client too early, they may not be able to take it in and might actually retreat from the therapy. We need to really be sure what the client is communicating, and this might take time.

Case vignettes

Angela

Angela, a West Indian client in her late thirties, came to therapy to discuss her anxiety. It had become generalized into different areas of her life, and one of her main concerns was that it was preventing her from going out of the house and interacting with other people. Early on in the therapy, she revealed that she had been sexually abused by a member of her own culture. She often reported dreams featuring intruders, but she had not made the emotional connection to the earlier events in her life. One of these dreams was about a white man who came into her house and attempted to enter her bedroom; she tried to stop him, and after a difficult struggle he quickly entered her room and stole her bed cover, records, and other personal belongings. She remembered him as having a "distinctly English appearance". When she reported the dream, she was confused because the man was of another race. We slowly explored what it meant and we were able to unravel how she linked the childhood abuse with her experience of racism during the same week. This enabled us to explore what it meant to be in a cross-cultural therapeutic relationship. Initially, she had told me she did not mind what type of therapist she consulted or "whether they were black or white". However, at this stage, it was clear that I was seen as white. When I addressed this in the therapy, she felt embarrassed and wondered what I would think of her. She felt she was being ungrateful for the help she was receiving. I told her I thought it would actually be important for our work together to think about what it meant to be working with someone she did not perceive as "black". It was a step closer to exploring our relationship and her own ambivalence about needing support, but being frightened as to whether I would understand her experiences, since I belonged to another race and culture. She had West Indian roots, but was born and brought up in Britain, while I was brought up in three differ- ent countries. The client also needs to know that their own culture will not be criticized as a result of their own critique and disap- pointment with the behaviour of another member of their culture, as in this client's case. She had to build up a lot of trust to disclose this to me, as it was something she had held as a secret.

Angela experienced racism, but the sexual abuse was actually perpetrated by a man from her own culture. However, in the dream there is an amalgamation of events. Moreover, this reflects the complexity of the transference when racial/cultural factors come into play. The therapist may not be seen only as a parental figure, but as a representative of a cultural group, either the client's or as part of another culture. In Angela's case, for a brief period, I became part of the dominant culture. All of these components have to be unravelled slowly in the process of the therapy.

Stella

Stella, a Greek client in her thirties, was referred to me because her Greek doctor thought she needed to see a Greek therapist. She had been diagnosed as "clinically depressed" by her doctor and put on antidepressant medication. She made an appointment to see me, in the most resentful way, feeling pushed into something she herself had ambivalent ideas about. It did not take long for her to fight the therapy, saying how she was too busy for therapy, that she had attended as it was respectful to turn up to the session, but seemed extremely ambivalent about the whole process and what might emerge. She was very curious about me; as soon as our first session had finished she got up to leave, but then, to my surprise, was full of questions, such as whether I was married to a Greek, or whether I was born in Greece or here, and if so, where. Of course, I did not answer these questions, but suggested that in the next meeting we think about the meanings of all of her questions, as I suspected she had a lot more on her mind about culture and roots. In the next meeting, once again she wanted to know whether I was a "fully- fledged member" of the culture, and told me how long she had been in the UK and how proud she was that she no longer had any trace of an accent, unlike other Greeks. When I explored the language issue with her, she said she would rather speak only in English, even stating her name in the Anglicized way. Not surprisingly with this level of negative transference to the Greek culture, projected towards me, she terminated the therapeutic relationship after a few sessions.

However, less than one year later Stella returned, requesting further help. Now she felt it was *her* choice to continue this process. I had wondered whether the referring GP was a bit like her father, whom she always described as a bully. He was also the one that had decided to uproot them all to the UK. She had felt pushed into this culture and now she needed to be the instigator of her own experiences (which manifested itself in other ways in her life). She held a multitude of stereotypes about what I would be like, and it all felt too close. I felt she also saw me as a potential bully, although, in fact, what was out of her awareness was how she could turn it around and behave like the bully. All these dynamics had to be discussed, out in the open, and it took her by surprise. She always saw herself as the victim, so became rather surprised when we began to look at how she could also throw aggression at others. This had become a protective mechanism, but was nevertheless operative. She slowly enabled herself to have an experience of me that challenged her view of the Greek bully father, but also the Greek woman that would behave like her family, in fact like her mentally ill mother. I found out that her mother had been hospitalized with a breakdown aged thirty, shortly after Stella's birth.

She was the youngest of three children, the other two being boys. She imagined that her mother just could not cope with a girl and had many stories of how "the boys (referring to her brothers) got away with murder", and she laughed. Of course, culturally, she was probably right that they were treated differently, but they all had experienced a depressed mother who was physically and psychologically absent for much of their childhood. Interestingly, there was usually a sense of humour when describing the depression. This affect was not only inappropriate, but it showed me how she had become so used to making it all a joke in order to expel the painful and unbearable feelings towards mother, but also her siblings, whom she viewed as always having an easier time. She said for years, her way of being was to be the Greek woman who did not have needs, as having any needs would be like her father, who was controlling her, or her mother, who was completely out of control. When these conversations took place, interestingly enough, I realized I no longer seemed Greek to her as she was describing something in great detail as if I would not understand. In fact, she laughed after one revelation, saying with great relief how "she had forgotten I was Greek". It was as if the realization came back to her like a thunderbolt and she had to sit up straight and behave, as she had had to do when she was growing up.

We worked together for a total of three years, at all times being mindful of her need of space and supporting her to distance herself from the Greek mother who took up all her internal feeling and thinking. A few months after her mother died (which was during the therapeutic treatment), she was describing something and slipped into the Greek pronunciation of "Stella". She looked at me, concerned, and I commented on what she might be expecting to see or hear. She paused and said she expected me to correct her as her mother would have done, and which meant she was always on guard. Her eyes then filled with tears, and it slowly opened up the whole area of how she had alienated herself from anything positive from the Greek culture because of her mother. She now felt free to reclaim something of her culture that she *chose* to have.

In conclusion, the cultural background, experiences, values, and attitudes influence the psychological processes for both the client and the therapist. The therapist cannot claim that he or she is culturally neutral, and instead, it is vital that therapists have awareness of their own culture and its impact on their development before working with someone of a different culture or race. As Thomas states,

> Claiming neutrality on the therapist's part puts the client in a diffi-cult position because the therapist has thereby divested herself/himself of those things that might connect with the client's culture and background, be this positively or otherwise. A therapist who claims cultural neutrality also robs the client of the opportunity to speculate or to make observations about the therapist's background, particularly if this has an effect on the therapy in terms of connection or fit. [1995, p. 172]

References

Acquarone, S. (2004). *Infant–Parent Psychotherapy: A Handbook*. London: Karnac.

Akhtar, S. (2006). Technical challenges faced by the immigrant psychoanalyst. *Psychoanalyic Quarterly*, 75: 21–43.

Chin, J. L. (1994). Psychodynamic approaches. In: L. Comas-Diaz & B. Greene (Eds.), *Women of Color: Integrating Ethnic and Gender Identities in Psychotherapy* (pp. 194–222). New York: Guilford Press.

Comas-Diaz, L., & Jacobsen, F. M. (1991). Ethnocultural transference and countertransference in the therapeutic dyad. *American Journal of Orthopsychiatry*, 61(3): 392–402.

Curry, A. (1964). Myth, transference and the black psychotherapist. *Psychoanalytic Review*, 51: 7–14.

Danueq, M. N.-A. (1988). *Willow Weep for Me: A Black Woman's Journey Through Depression*. New York: W. W. Norton.

Eleftheriadou, Z. (2006). Revisiting the concepts of racism and culture: some thoughts on the clinical implications. In: K. White (Ed.), *Unmasking Race, Culture and Attachment in the Psychoanalytic Space* (pp. 36–45). London: Karnac.

Freud, S. (1895d). *Studies on Hysteria*. S.E., 2: 253–306. London: Hogarth.

Holmes, D. E. (1992). Race and transference in psychoanalysis and psychotherapy. *International Journal of Psychoanalysis*, 73: 1–11.

Laird, J. (1998). Theorizing culture: narrative ideas and practice principles. In: M. McGoldrick (Ed.), *Re-Visioning Family Therapy: Race, Culture and Gender in Clinical Practice* (pp. 20–36). London: Guilford Press.

Liggan, D. Y., & Kay, J. (2006). Race in the room: issues in the dynamic psychotherapy of African Americans. In: R. Moodley & S. Palmer (Eds.), *Race, Culture and Psychotherapy*, (pp.100–115). London: Routledge.

Mishne, J. (2002). *Multiculturalism and the Therapeutic Process*. London: Guilford Press.

McGoldrick, M. (Ed.). (1998). *Re-Visioning Family Therapy: Race, Culture and Gender in Clinical Practice*. London: Guilford Press.

Mukherjee, B. (1999). Imagining homelands. In: A. Aciman (Ed.). *Letters of Transit: Reflections on Exile, Identity, Language and Loss* (pp. 65–86). New York: New Press.

Samuels, A. (1993). *The Political Psyche*. London: Routledge.

Thomas, L. (1995). Psychotherapy in the context of race and culture: an inter-cultural therapy approach. In: S. Fernando (Ed.), *Mental Health in a Multi-Ethnic* Society (pp. 172–190). London: Routledge.

Tuckwell, G. (2006). Psychodynamic counselling, "race" and culture. In: S. Wheeler (Ed.), *Difference and Diversity in Counselling* (pp. 137–155). New York: Palgrave.

Winnicott, D. (1967). Mirror-role of mother and family in child development. In: P. Lomas (Ed.). *The Predicament of the Family: A Psychoanalytic Symposium* (pp. 111–118). London: Hogarth Press.

CHAPTER FOUR

Barriers to cross-cultural work

Zack Eleftheriadou

T his chapter will outline potential barriers to cross-cultural work and some thoughts on how to work with them. The setting, verbal communication (such as working in another language or working with interpreters), non-verbal communication, direct/indirect style of communication, and the variation of emotional expression across cultures will be examined.

The organization

Careful planning has to take place to determine a "good-enough" location for a cross-cultural therapy service, and whether one is aiming to serve a particular community group. Although there is not an ideal location to serve all communities, a centre should be near the communities it aims to serve, and yet not too central to the community. Discretion is essential, as for some communities there is embarrassment and shame about coming to therapy, fears that they are going "mad", or in some cases they can really be alienated from the family and community for seeking outside support (Lago & Thomson, 1996).

Some thought needs to be given to how to make a setting welcoming to those of different backgrounds. Visual images and décor have to be chosen carefully, reflecting the client group(s). More notably, the staff team, to a large extent, will be seen as potential role models and as holding a certain level of power and authority. If the team is predominantly white, then it will give a particular message about race, culture (and even class and gender dynamics) to the clients. Furthermore, their reputation for liaising with community groups, traditional healers, and religious leaders, among others, quickly becomes known (see "External section" for further discussion of networking).

There are some key questions we need to ask ourselves: what is our client's transference to the organization / setting? At times, it is useful to be explicit about these first feelings, such as saying something to the client such as, "What did you imagine about the therapeutic organization and who [referring to the therapist] you would see today?" This is an exploration to find out something about their past and present significant attachments, but also, racially, what their perceptions are. For example, is the new therapeutic setting perceived as a predominantly "white/black" organization, a culturally foreign environment, or other associations they may have. The decorations on the walls and the books and magazines in the waiting room all communicate something as well as what the client will project (or place their own unconscious meanings, which may have nothing to do with the reality) on to them. The suggestion here is not to have bare walls and waiting areas, as I believe that provides a very clinical environment, but rather an awareness of our choices and what they might represent to our clients.

Cross-cultural consultants have noted how the administrative staff of therapy/mental health centres sometimes feel a need to fill the gap for "lost cultures". They project to the clients the missing parts of their cultures to try to regain them for their personal unresolved loss. One administrative member, whom I interviewed in a team support meeting, spoke of her strong wish to provide the children with objects to make up for their losses. She spoke about a particular client, a Caribbean child whom she had spoken to about music from his "home" island and knew she had overstepped her administrative role. She later admitted how uncomfortable she felt seeing him come to the centre with his white foster parent, knowing that his black father was absent, "to help get to know his roots". Of course, for the child, this would not have been helpful in any way, and would have slotted this child into an identity he did not possess. It is equally important to understand these types of projections and make them more conscious to the referrer, so they do not interfere with the work. I have encountered mental health referrers who had (sometimes unconscious) views on which type of therapist the child "should" work with. These are delicate issues that require careful consideration in formalized staff meetings. Workers drawn to work in such settings are often reminded of their own issues.

Non-verbal communication

Anyone who has completed any type of observational exercise, but particularly an infant observation (which is, nowadays, increasingly part of both child and adult therapy trainings), will know that there is a huge volume of non-verbal communication and we also rely on transference and countertransference communication (see Chapter Three). We have come to depend so much on the verbal mode of communication that we often feel quite deskilled when we are unable to work with someone who speaks a different language. Infant observation teaches us the importance of patience and waiting to understand something as it unfolds. When you tune into an infant, you slowly find out how they feel, also by utilizing refined countertransference reactions and feelings to understand the unconscious communications and how they influence us and we influence them.

We can only bring ourselves into the consulting room, and our clients will notice our facial expressions and body language, whether we intend to convey these signals or not. In any communication, there is a type of synchronization or dance that takes place between members, and, of course, the more "tuned in" members are to each other, the more synchronized it appears to the observer. Lago and Thomson (1996) bring to our attention how young children seem to be able to communicate and synchronize with children from other cultures, but how this changes with development as signals and movement patterns become more culturally informed. Our stance, as well as the consulting room layout, will reflect our ideas on personal and interpersonal space. Physical proximity between the therapist and client will vary depending on individual attachment patterns, gender, and the particular cultural norms. These include eye contact, physical proximity, forms of address, behaviours, and gestures that we feel comfortable with. For example (generally speaking and by no means all), Latin Americans tend to shake hands for longer and in a more vigorous way, or, as another example, in most cultures we use the right hand, but, interestingly, in Muslim cultures offering someone something with the left hand may be interpreted as offensive. The left hand is considered "unclean" and is not used for food intake. We have to be comfortable with these issues, as a client from another culture may appear over-familiar to someone who is not used to a closer physical proximity. Most of these behaviours are not consciously thought about (as discussed in further detail in Chapter Two), but the therapist has to be open and expect to encounter variations.

Language

Learning to speak another language is an intricate process. One can learn the actual words, but being able to communicate properly goes far beyond that, because one has to understand the paralinguistic. This means the manner in which language comes across, which includes learning the tone, expression, subtle cues, pauses, sighs, silences, accent, pitch, and volume. It is interesting that people assume that they are communicating in English and they have an understanding, but as D'Ardenne and Mahtani remind us,

> There are many forms of English in the world . . . counsellors expect their clients to share their manner of speech. When they do not, counsellors may devalue their clients, either by believing they are intellectually slow or that they are uneducated. [1990, p. 64]

Sociological studies (see Bernstein, 1958, 1961) have shown us how some people speak in context-dependent ways, shown through many dialects and formed as a way of having intra-community dialogues that create a separate identity. Class and education produce "alternative forms of English". The only way to understand the meanings is to know the context. Some educational establishments have taken this on board, and there are working groups on how to improve the educational achievement of ethnic minorities, aiming to improve expression and writing in English.

We often forget that most clients who have to communicate distressing events find it difficult to express this in another language. Expression does not emerge as fluently as they would wish, so words and meanings change. Not surprisingly, people often report that they sound less friendly and less intelligent when speaking another language. So, the overall experience is often that of alienation, frustration, and anger because of not being able to get the "intended" meaning across. Furthermore, knowing that they are speaking to the authority may be extremely inhibiting and can also make their spoken (and thinking) English deteriorate. Power inequalities in relationships are relayed through subtle language, and if the relationship is unequal, then the communication is not authentic. As Lago and Thomson suggest,

> The culturally different client is likely to suffer indirect discrimination as a consequence of being misunderstood . . . both parties tend to judge the other's behaviour in terms of criteria which they do not share and do not verbalize. [1996, p. 65]

From a psychoanalytic perspective, it is interesting that not only Freud (for example, in his famous clinical cases of Dora and the Wolf Man), but many other early psychoanalysts, such as Karl Abraham, Theodore Reik, Alfred Adler, and Sandor Rado, practised psychoanalysis in different languages to their own mother tongue and/or that of their patients, and yet it still remains an area with relatively little literature. Ferenczi (1989) was the first to keep a written account of his observations when working in languages other than the mother tongue. He noted in his observations that clients could pronounce obscene words without the inhibition shown by those using mother tongue words.

Jimenez (2004) raises the difference between the words "translation" and "interpretation", and suggests we are doing both during the therapy. There is a level of translating or "fidelity" (*ibid.*, p. 1368) to the text/client's narrative, and, of course, another level, the interpretative, where we have to go beyond the literal meaning, go to the more "symbolic" (Rycroft, 1968) meaning and let our mind wonder. The latter, more interpretative level, implies experiencing countertransference feelings (see Chapter Three), which includes the thera-pist's feelings, triggered by the client's issues. The client's material may be too unbearable for them to consider, and they unconsciously pass it on to the therapist to think about, or as if to hold on to them. In other words, the therapist's interpretative state is that of holding on to unconscious ideas. These ideas might seem senseless or frag-mented at the time, but will make sense eventually. By doing so, Jimenez demonstrates through clinical work that there can be a pro-found understanding in this cross-cultural work, precisely because one is so sensitive to the "literal meanings of words, meanings that have ceased being conscious for a person who has mastered the language from childhood". He goes on to say, "I wonder if being in analysis with a foreigner does not render more likely the emergence in the transference of unheard-of, rejected aspects that have been set aside and projected far away" (2004, p. 1371; see also Argentieri and Canestri [1993]).

The therapeutic relationship relies largely on the pre-verbal and emotional level of communication. Despite the feelings of many clients who may reject a therapist who is not fluent in their mother tongue, and sceptics of cross-cultural work, there can be a deep connection between the two people, or what Stern (1985) calls "affect attunement". According to Jimenez, this connection is as a result of a "continuous exchange process" and results in "progres-sive sharpening of verbal communication" (2004, p. 1374). What is also interesting is that Jimenez (2004) draws on Stern's (1985) research and speculates that, like infants who demonstrate "amodal perception" (or the ability to take in information in one sensory modality and translate it into another), the cross-cultural therapist is also able to engage in this process. This implies that the therapist is able to match, or be in touch with, the client's affective state, although they do not have to use the same mode as the client. So, emotional expressions are expressed in different modes by the client and therapist, but they are able to find a connection. Of course, this takes a skilled professional who has done a great deal of personal work in the cross-cultural field and is able to monitor and reflect on their conscious and unconscious emotional reactions.

I cannot emphasize enough "that learning about a culture is not the same as experiencing it" (Amati-Mehler, 1995, p. 3). Further-more, Amati-Mehler reminds us that

When a child first learns the names of things, the link between the image of an object and the word that indicates it also includes affects in the memory trace. It is this intersection of affects, cognition, and speech that defences such as repression and/or splitting can influence language. [*ibid.*]

So, if one of our clients has learnt the language as a result of emigration, it will be a different psychic experience, with a different intensity of meaning, to that of child who learnt it at home or during their schooling. Coming into contact with a second language can be enriching and creative, as the English writer, Samuel Beckett, found when he chose to move away to France, where he found the freedom to write through French (Antinucci, 2004). For others, being away from their mother tongue can be an alienating or even traumatic experience. The meaning attached to a new language will also depend on the family's attitudes towards learning/speaking another language (see Chapter Five). We know that cross-cultural conflicts in the parents can end up being expressed by their children.

During the therapeutic process, we have the luxury of exploring creatively; we can literally play with words, refine them along the way, and go over meanings again and again. It is such a useful exercise to try to get as close as possible to what the other means; even if we just unpick one single sentence, we find there are multiple meanings which can be potentially misconstrued and misunderstood (Spinelli, 1989; Van Deurzen-Smith, 1988).

Working in a second language brings its own challenges. For some clients, it frees them to discuss topics that are difficult for them culturally, and for others it becomes simply too difficult. What is interesting for us, as therapists, is that early material may not be accessed so easily if communicated in their non-mother tongue or fluent language.

Style of communication

In some cultures, there is more emphasis on direct communication, which is considered "focused" and direct, but in other cultures this may be experienced as "abrasive" and "rude". In yet other cultures, indirect and softly spoken communication is preferred, as it is thought to be less confrontational, but by others again can be perceived to be less assertive, even "shy" or evasive in terms of the questions, challenges, or topics explored. In one context, a son may be expected to look at his father with eyes of respect, and in another quite the opposite. Another common issue is around assertiveness, where, in some cultures, for example, Southern European countries, you are expected to offer something more than once, even if refused. It may be considered rather impolite not to accept. In North American and Northern European countries this is experienced as "pushy" and not listening to them properly. These issues need some thinking about, as refusing a client's gift is not straightforward, as was illustrated when a young Greek client's mother insisted on sending me food, via her daughter, who was in therapy suffering from an eating disorder (bulimia). Interestingly, her daughter kept "forgetting" to bring me this "gift from her mother" over a few weeks. I had to examine with her both the cultural and the psychological meanings of this gift.

Verbal communication is valued more in Western countries and there is less tolerance for silence (and, hence, it can be very difficult for people to get used to having silences in therapy). The culture and rules of therapy sometimes have to be made explicit so that clients do not feel they are behaving "oddly". Clients are probably feeling alienated enough in terms of their distress that confusion over the meanings of the therapy setting can push them further into a state of "aloneness".

All societies have ways of dealing with emotions. A vivid example that comes to mind is from some years back, when the Italian actor, Roberto Benini, won an Oscar for the moving film *Life is Beautiful*; he was very explicit and public about his emotions. A British actor who appeared on stage just after Benini described in his speech how he was not displaying it, but was experiencing what Benini had demonstrated, but it was on the "inside". This vignette shows us how cultures may favour certain kinds of emotions, that is, encourage positive ones more than their negative counterparts. It is important that we do not interpret behaviour at face value. Sue and Sue (1990) give many similar examples, such as that of Asian Americans, who value restraint of strong feelings and any personal information is shared only with close family members.

Social psychology has provided us with plenty of research examples to illustrate the differences in emotional expression, such as the dramatic findings in a study by Friesen (1972), which are still applicable for us today. Friesen chose to test Japanese and American students who were shown short films; one was a film about body mutilation, which was to produce anxiety, and the other was a neutral film. In Scenario 1, the films were shown to them on their own, and in Scenario 2, they were shown the films with a "scientist" present. When they were on their own, both sets of students exhibited similar emotions, including disgust at the non-neutral film. However, the surprise occurred when the "scientist" was present, as the Japanese response was very different; they seemed less disgusted and even smiled more. The study presents evidence for why the Japanese display spontaneous emotions created in the presence of someone else. In this case, the "authenticity" evoked (perhaps) an appropriate social response, rather than what the subjects experienced. This study, among others, illustrates that it is not necessarily that people from other cultures do not experience the same emotions or with the same intensity. Often, behaviour is used as a guide or predictor of someone's culture or relationship to that culture. Behaviour itself cannot be a guide to an individual's relationship to culture. Culture includes all the more subtle patterns of relating that are simply not visible.

Working with interpreters

Often, it is not possible to have a therapist from exactly the same cultural context and we have to find *suitable* interpreters to bridge the gaps. That is, it is paramount that they are able take on board the nature of therapeutic work and exactly what is expected from them. Ideally, they need to have undertaken a course in counselling work to understand what it entails: for example, allowing silences and not intervening with their own opinions. Whenever time allows, it is useful to meet with interpreters briefly before a session and, equally, to have time to debrief afterwards; this has been useful as there might be a signal they suddenly remember, or I am aware that they found something uncomfortable and wanted to "protect" the client or the culture, or did not want to embarrass the client by really saying what they had said, so they changed it slightly. These meetings are fruitful and can also help to prevent the interpreter from taking away difficult emotional material.

I have worked with clients directly, even though they were struggling in English, and with others where I have had to use interpreters. Both scenarios have been difficult, and, at times, slower than the normal pace of the work. The flow of the communication depends on the interpreter and their psychological knowledge and ability to bear the client's emotional process. The right interpreter can enhance the communication and bridge the language gap. They can be extremely informative on cultural information and bring hope to the process, which can facilitate the client to receive support from a stranger. If it is the case that they identify with the interpreter and feel that they are part of the setting, trust is increased. However, I have also encountered the scenario of a male interpreter who was assigned (in the absence of his female colleague) to a Somali client who had a history of sexual abuse. Despite the therapist's hesitancy, the session went ahead (with the client's consent, of course), and it proved difficult. The client provided some basic information, but in the most minimal, non-emotional way possible. Afterwards, the interpreter thought the session had gone well, but to the therapist the client still seemed rather polite and withdrawn. The therapist had to make a decision about the interpreter and decided to follow her gut feeling and not invite this man back for another meeting. The client then cancelled the following meeting, but then was invited back for a second assessment, emphasizing that this would take place alongside a female interpreter. This was felt to be a completely different session; the dynamics between them seemed to have a flavour of a grandmother–granddaughter relationship. Therapeutically, this was extremely helpful, as the mother spoke about desperate feelings of needing support parenting her newborn. As shown by this example, even though they shared a culture and religion, discussing difficult gender issues in front of a male is inappropriate for some cultural groups. Therefore, it is not always easy to find the right match of interpreter and client. They have to be matched in that they really do share a language or dialect, and also that politically they can sit in the same room. Additionally, one has to allow for the possibility for a time when the client's English improves and they can work without an interpreter, or they simply do not need the physiological comfort of someone from the same culture/language group.

In another situation, I was working with a woman from an Arab country with an interpreter. One day, the interpreter was unable to attend, and I made the decision to try to work with her anyway. It was difficult for her, but with her broken English and my broken French we were able to have a "good enough" connection. Towards the end of the session, I asked her how she had felt and how different our meeting had been without an interpreter, and she was very clear that we could do without, and how it was possible for me to understand her. She told me how difficult it had been for her in the UK, as people "quickly gave up on her". She was relaying these emotions in terms of language, but it turned out to be a strong belief of hers that people just persevere to see things through. I had to work hard to earn any trust from her, and this was more evident when there was no longer a third party present. Eventually, we were able to work together for the next two years without an interpreter.

Who exactly is the client?

It is more common that clients from extended family cultural backgrounds (often from Asian and Southern Mediterranean populations) attend therapy accompanied by family members. This is a regular occurrence with clients from more communal types of backgrounds, or those who are new to therapy. If is the first session, I would not assume I am just going to work with the individual. I would have some flexibility, either to invite the other person to join me in the consulting room or to ask the person referred whether they would prefer to come into the consulting room on their own. It is necessary to find out what their relationship is to that other person and how they feel with them remaining outside. I have encountered both scenarios, and, of course, there is no easy solution; the difficulty is listening to the unconscious communications about the person accompanying them. There have been other therapeutic scenarios where the husband or a sister has remained outside in the waiting room, as a support in the journey to therapy and back. Even if they are not in the room, it can feel as if they are part of the process, and this has to be addressed.

Case example

Anna

Anna, a Bulgarian woman, came with her husband and four-year-old boy to talk about concerns about her son's behaviours, especially sleeping patterns. Her husband came along and sat in silence. I tried to engage him, but I experienced him as distant. He said it was better for his wife to explain, as her English was better. The only thing he wished to share was that he was a builder and hardly at home, and she worked part-time in an office, as a secretary. I acknowledged the language issue, but still thought he could contribute to the conversation, and I encouraged him to try to add to our discourse. I kept him in mind, and noted his body language, which seemed to be that of someone extremely uncomfortable and who wanted to curl up in the corner. I realized later that not only it is essential to explore whether they wish to be involved, but also what is the particular dynamic being communicated about the family. They sat with the little boy in between them, and I had such a strong countertransference of this father being "kept out", just like his statement of being a busy builder and working long hours. The mother wished to treat me as she would talk to her sister and "keep the men out", as she said with shy laughter. The shyness was due to some embarrassment, as she also kept him out of their bed, replacing him with her son. There were clearly no boundaries with the four-year-old, as he was trying to open the door and get out of the room, empty the contents of her purse (which embarrassed the mother), and generally not allow his parents to engage in any conversation.

They agreed to come back for another meeting, but at the next appointment it was just her with her son. In a way, they were like a couple, and it was her opportunity to talk about how unhappy she was with her husband. She told me that he had an affair some years back and years later she just could not forgive him. We had several sessions together and then she called to cancel, saying she had been unwell. After uncertainty about whether they had received our letter, I rang them and had the opportunity to speak to him, and invited him back with her. To my surprise, he came along. His English was better than I had thought. It was evident that the marital problems were being expressed through the boy and they actually needed couple therapy. Eventually, they agreed to attend without their son. In any therapy, the father has to be kept in mind, as they will be contributing to the psychological makeup of the family. We looked at different possibilities with this family, even how their family could be, and talked about how their family or cultural patterns were not "set in stone", as they had initially presented. The process took some time, as it was, in fact, the father who seemed relieved with the idea of becoming more involved and being needed, while the mother seemed more hesitant, carrying images of her authoritative father.

In conclusion, it is important to give thought to the possible barriers that we cannot remove, but we can learn to think about them with our clients. Often, they might be presented as barriers, so that we do not go into any discussion about them. It is not about getting the geography or the landscape of the therapeutic service absolutely right, but simply being sensitive to all the possible individual, familial, and cultural meanings. Even if the layout of the room reflects a particular way of thinking, this can be verbalized and we can see what meaning it holds for the client. Therapists are often so concerned that they will offend the client because they do not know the "appropriate cultural norms", but if the therapist is open-minded, and has a space for the other culture that is respectful, then he/she can find out from the client more information *regarding when and if it is necessary* and work with it (see Eleftheriadou, 1996). As Mishne, quite wisely, reminds us,

A lack of knowledge, combined with a spirit of enquiry, can be an asset. It can facilitate dialogue and sharing of expectations, beliefs and customs, and can demonstrate a therapist's willingness to learn about and to respect a patient's perspective. [2002, p. 118]

References

Amati-Mehler, J. (1995). The exiled language. *Canadian Journal of Psychoanalysis*, 3: 87–104.

Antinucci, P. (2004). I need to hide in my forgiveness. Will you forgive me? In: I. Ward & J. Szekacs-Weisz (Eds.), *Lost Childhood and the Language of Exile* (pp. 66–75). London: Imago/The Freud Museum.

Argentieri, S., & Canestri, J. (1993). *The Babel of the Unconscious. Mother Tongue and Foreign Languages in the Psychoanalytic Dimension.* Madison, CT: International University Press.

Bernstein, B. (1958). Some sociological determinants of perception: an enquiry into sub-cultural differences. *British Journal of Sociology (London), 9*: 159–174.

Bernstein, B. (1961). Social class and linguistic development: a theory of social learning. In: A. H. Halsey, J. Floud, & C. A. Anderson (Eds.), *Education, Economy and Society* (pp. 288–314). New York: Free Press.

D'Ardenne, P., & Mahtani, A. (1990). *Transcultural Counselling.* London: Sage.

Eleftheriadou, Z. (1996). Skills for communicating with patients from different cultural backgrounds. In: R. Bor & M. Lloyd (Eds.), *Communication Skills for Medicine* (pp. 85–105). Edinburgh: Churchill Livingstone.

Ferenczi, S. (1989). *The Clinical Diary.* M. Balint & N. Z. Jackson (Trans.). Cambridge, MA: Harvard University Press.

Friesen, W. (1972). Cultural differences in facial expressions in a social situation: an experimental test of the concept of display rules. Unpublished PhD thesis. San Francisco, CA, University of California.

Jimenez, J. P. (2004). Between the confusion of tongues and the gift of tongues: or working with a psychoanalyst in a foreign language. *International Journal of Psychoanalysis, 85*: 1365–1377.

Lago, C., & Thomson, J. (1996). *Race, Culture, and Counselling.* Buckingham: Open University Press.

Mishne, J. (2002). *Multiculturalism and the Therapeutic Process.* London: Guilford Press.

Rycroft, C. (1968). A *Critical Dictionary of Psychoanalysis.* London: Penguin.

Spinelli, E. (1989). *The Interpreted World: An Introduction to Phenomenological Psychology.* London: Sage.

Stern, D. (1985). *The Interpersonal World of the Infant.* New York: Basic Books.

Sue, D. W., & Sue, D. (1990). *Counselling the Culturally Different.* New York: Wiley.

Van Deurzen-Smith, E. (1988). *Existential Counselling in Practice.* London: Sage.

CHAPTER FIVE

Clinical assessment

Zack Eleftheriadou

T his chapter provides information on the first meeting of the therapist and client. Although many of the therapeutic issues are connected to the next chapter, it is believed that the first session is so important to how the scene is set for the therapy and the therapeutic relationship that it warrants special attention. If the client has a positive experience from the first meeting(s), they are more likely to return and engage in further therapeutic work.

During the assessment stage or initial sessions, information is gathered which may indicate the potential course of the therapeutic relationship. The first meeting can be used to find out about the client's world, their trust in people, and what are their significant intimate attachments (past and present), which includes family history, parenting experiences, and relationship with siblings, significant current or past losses, relationship history, parenting (if applicable). Furthermore, we could be interested in their work and educational history and whether their familial/parental job/careers led them to particular areas (consciously or unconsciously). Additionally, one can establish if there is any psychiatric history and any medication in the present or past, any link with other mental health services, and contact with other related agencies. A therapist can find herself trying to balance obtaining enough background information with, at the same time, leaving room for the relationship to unfold at its own pace. Some therapists send a questionnaire beforehand, but many prefer to wait to meet the patient and let their history unfold in the course of the sessions. It is important to take a good history, however, as this may be difficult once the therapy progresses; one does not want to interrupt with questions as it disrupts the flow of the communication (particularly unconscious communication).

Our clients often come to us for support at a time when they need help with "psychic survival", owing to a profound distress at that particular point in their lives. Of course, if the reasons are not clear, then it is essential to wonder why they have sought therapy at *that particular point in time* (Bateman & Holmes, 1995). They will bring all their anxieties, hopes, and fears, but it is important to acknowledge that the very fact that they have decided to get in touch with someone implies there is some hope for change (Cooper & Alfille, 2005). The therapist has the delicate stance of remaining professional, but being emotionally connected. This is a rather delicate balance to achieve, particularly as the first session can be quite "emotionally loaded" (we may get a whistle-stop tour of many of the client's themes, but not necessarily a great deal of clarity or detail about their emotion; this comes with time). The therapeutic space is also a cultural space where potential projections will emerge, ethnic identities will be explored, and (internal and external) racial stressors will come up. The therapist will formulate ideas regarding the client's needs, but always keeping an open mind that these may be wrong formulations or only "bits" of the story. Alongside the narrative, a useful tool is to be aware of what s/he represents to the client, as well as his/her countertransference responses and how these change throughout the therapy. No therapist is neutral once they have heard about or met their client; from the moment they meet, they form conscious and unconscious ideas about each other. According to Tonnesmann, "It is the patient who has the opportunity to decide afresh whether he wants psychotherapy, and it is the therapist who will have to decide whether the patient needs psychotherapy" (2005, p. xi).

Apart from the above general assessment issues, there are further ones to consider with someone from a different culture.

After all, their concept of counselling or therapy may be not as clear, since they are newcomers to the culture, or share a different cultural lens. For example, these individuals may not have had any friends who have been for counselling or psychotherapy, or have images of these through the media, as one would see in many western countries. Grieger and Ponterotto (1995) outline six cross-cultural components, which are useful to consider during the assessment stage and can be kept in mind alongside the issues mentioned thus far. These include:

> The client's level of psychological mindedness (defined as familiarity with the western middle-class conception of the term), the family's level of psychological mindedness, the client's/family's attitude toward counseling, the client's level of acculturation, the family's level of acculturation, and the family's attitude toward acculturation. [*ibid.*, p. 360]

The above components are extremely useful, but perhaps it is more useful to think about the "type" of individual and family psychological mindedness rather than the "level" of psychological mindedness. The reason for this is that clients from different cultures have a *different* way of conceptualizing about emotions and interactions rather than possessing a higher or lower level of psychological mindedness. This has often been used as a case against the provision of cross-cultural therapy services to ethnic minorities.

Individual type of psychological mindedness

The first assessment factor, the individual's type of psychological mindedness, includes all the ways individuals conceptualize or make an assessment about their emotional state. This would indicate whether they had a choice about, or understood, the referral, whether they attribute the distress to biological or psychological factors, whether they manifest their difficulties/distress bodily or verbally, and, generally, how these fit within the client's sociocultural construct. This point also poses the question of how much therapists need to inform the client about psychological constructs.

At times, a client may find it useful to have names (this does not imply psychiatric categories, although, undoubtedly, I have encountered clients who are so relieved to have their distress "named", even if it comes under a psychiatric category; and they may not even be aware of all the implications of a psychiatric label) for their distress and ways that it can be worked with. It is important to emphasize here a type of flexibility as essential in the naming, a more descriptive way, and an open-ended questioning manner.

Type of familial psychological mindedness

Second, and similarly to the individual's type of psychological mindedness, the type of familial psychological mindedness requires investigation. When clients and their families have different notions of distress, it is likely to increase conflict. Manifestation of distress can be examined cross-culturally along the two polarities of what has been called "psychologization" or "somatization". An example of the former would be western, commonly used words for "depression" and "anxiety". Instead, Yoruba people refer to these concepts through bodily states, such as "the heart is weak", or "the heart is not at rest" (Leff, 1988).

The client's/family's attitude towards therapy

Third, the client's/family's attitude towards therapy will have an impact on the therapeutic outcome. Grieger and Ponterotto provide the example of Irish-American families:

> There is a cultural value on stoicism, on keeping a stiff upper lip, and on not "feeling sorry" for oneself. In a family of this background, an individual who is depressed and trying to express that as a psychological or emotional phenomenon may receive little support . . . For a client from a background in which the family does not believe in emotional disturbance or psychological explanations for unhappiness, entering the therapeutic process may be conflictual. [1995, p. 363]

Acculturation issues

The fourth point, on acculturation issues, refers to how much the client has incorporated the dominant culture (see Chapter Two, pp. 23–24). For example, whether their choice of partner, social groups, or support systems includes people of the same culture or of different cultures, how would the community judge them as successful or unsuccessful, among other information? The relationship to one's culture can be used as an indication of how much the client accepts or rejects culture, and, therefore, how much they will engage in the therapeutic process with a therapist of another culture. If there is too much distance, the therapeutic relationship may not work successfully. According to Grieger and Ponterotto the research results "indicate that levels of acculturation and ethnic identity development are related to client's attitudes toward Western-type mental health services and to levels of mental health functioning" (*ibid.*, p. 359).

There are times when it is sufficient for a client to know that the therapist is also a member of the same or another culture to that of the majority culture, because they feel it gives them a closer connection and a better understanding of their experience. Some clients may be threatened by contact with someone from an overtly different background. An example may be a (strongly religious) Muslim woman who does not wish to work with a male therapist, or a Muslim man being alone with a female therapist. These are obvious mismatches (in terms of race or religion), which create conflict from the beginning. These are factual, or may also be imagined differences. Of course, the opposite can also take place, where it may be safer to confide to someone of another culture because the fears of someone being connected to their family or community are relatively limited. This may mean extra assurance regarding confidentiality will be required. An example is when working with Muslim girls, where any potential leakage of material means not only community gossip, but possible ostracism or punishment from their family or cultural group.

One of the significant things to keep in mind under this section is also how people pronounce their names, and it is worth mastering this. In my experience, some slightly more acculturated clients may go by their Anglicized names (which they often give to make it easier for the enquirer), but it is not necessarily what they identify with. Names are so profound that it is quite significant to try to get some sense of the affect and meanings they hold. I remember in one of the first sessions with one of my female Arab clients that I did not catch her name, so I asked her to repeat her name slowly until I could pronounce it properly. The atmosphere spoke volumes, much more than the actual words uttered, and I felt there was a real connection (Stern, 2004). She then told me several sessions later of being out with her friend, who had the repeated experience of being asked to repeat her name, and this led to more generalized comments that it was "too long" and that generally people gave up. I wondered about having to repeat her name with me, and I also asked her if it had a meaning. I was struck by the powerful meaning of her name and in sharing this with her, it made her burst into tears. She had a name akin to "hope", as she had been extremely premature and her parents thought they would lose her several times. She said that in her country people understand this, but in twenty years of living in the UK, she had never ever heard something positive about her name, adding "it was nice to hear something positive about it in English". Names and meanings around names are a very profound and creative route to significant cultural material. In my experience in telephone counselling work with both children and adults, they can also choose to use Anglicized names, which can sometimes reflect how much they have got used to their false self (see Thomas, 1995 for further discussion).

Family level of acculturation

The fifth factor, family level of acculturation, may provide indicators for the individual's relationships: for example, what language was or is currently spoken at home. Speaking to other colleagues, most clients are not asked what it is like to be speaking a language in therapy that is not your own, but that of the therapist (see Chapter Four for further discussion of linguistic issues). It is likely that those with even a trace of an accent have daily experiences of being noticed as being different, reinforced by subtle or more obvious prejudiced comments. So, the issue of language and what meaning it has in the therapeutic relationship needs thinking about. Other issues are whether cross-cultural friendships or partnerships are encouraged or discouraged.

The family's attitude towards acculturation

Last, the family's attitude towards acculturation can have an impact on the client's cultural identity. If the individual and familial ideas on acculturation are dissimilar, which include the type of engagement a client makes to the therapy; it can often be extremely stressful and become the focus of the therapy. This is common in people who have been brought up in the dominant culture. They may have learnt to speak the language and behave in ways that fit into what are considered "appropriate behaviours" of that culture, but they still hold another cultural pattern, which warrants exploration in the therapy.

All of the above ideas are a framework to keep in one's mind, and I do not want to give the impression of a busy therapist always asking questions, otherwise there would be no space for listening and following the client's particular path (which is interesting to follow any way; what they forget to tell us about or what they cannot stop mentioning, who are the protagonists of the story, and who gets a the small roles, etc.). In fact, questions should be used rather sparingly, and perhaps more so during the assessment process. However, it is interesting to see how the cross-cultural themes will emerge, particularly if we have them in mind and have given them adequate thought ourselves. Unconsciously, clients pick up cues from our tone and the particular words we choose to use, how much we know about cross-cultural issues and *how much we really want to know*. If they do not volunteer racial or cultural information, it is worth trying to explore this further with them. It has been my experience that this is often an uncomfortable topic, and yet holds such useful information. However, one cannot ask too many questions, as they are likely to be experienced as intrusive and can be problematic with issues of race and culture. They need to emerge in their own time and manner, within particular material (explicit or connected to other issues). The summary below lists the main areas that we can keep in mind in cross-cultural work, in order to ensure that significant subjects are not missed out.

In conclusion, the assessment process is important as it gives the client a taste of what therapy will be like (Bateman & Holmes, 1995). The way the client comes into the therapy, their way of making a connection to a new person and environment, the way they commit themselves or not, trust the other or not, among other behaviours, will tell us quite a lot about their past relationships and adaptation patterns. Grieger and Ponterotto's (1995) framework adds the cultural layer to the other general issues. In a way, they are all applicable to any client, whether from another culture or not (as they may still be unfamiliar with the whole culture of therapy and counselling). As emphasized earlier, the areas outlined are for therapists to keep in mind, rather than to cover explicitly or systematically with a client. Also, the process can be a long journey to examine the most intimate aspects of the clients and there can be much change as the therapy progresses (and, of course, as their life journey and relationships change). It is interesting to note that Bhugra and Bhui believe that: "omission of the ethnic, racial, linguistic, cultural as well as social class dimension will only manifest in a prolonged engagement phase" (2006, p. 51), implying being "stuck" in one phase of the therapy and not moving to deeper therapeutic, perhaps even more unconscious, work.

References

Bateman, A., & Holmes, J. (1995). *Introduction to Psychoanalysis*. London: Routledge.

Bhugra, D., & Bhui, K. (2006). Psychotherapy across the cultural divide. In: R. Moodley & S. Palmer (Eds.), *Race, Culture and Psychotherapy* (pp. 46–57). London: Routledge.

Cooper, J., & Alfille, H. (Eds.). (2005). *Assessment in Psychotherapy*. London: Karnac.

Grieger, I., & Ponterotto, J. G. (1995). A framework for assessment in multicultural counselling. In: J. G. Ponterotto, J. M. Casas, L. A. Suzuki, & C. M. Alexander (Eds.), *Handbook of Multicultural Counselling* (pp. 357–374). Thousand Oaks, CA: Sage.

Leff, J. (1988). *Psychiatry around the Globe*. London: Gaskell/Royal College of Psychiatrists.

Stern, D. (2004). *The Present Moment in Psychotherapy and Everyday Life*. London: Norton.

Thomas, L. (1995). Psychotherapy in the context of race and culture: an inter-cultural therapy approach. In: S. Fernando (Ed.), *Mental Health in a Multi-Ethnic Society* (pp. 172–190). London: Routledge.

Tonnesmann, M. (2005). Foreword. In: J. Cooper & H. Alfille (Eds.), *Assessment in Psychotherapy* (pp. ix–xii). London: Karnac.

CHAPTER SIX

The therapeutic relationship

Zack Elefetheriadou

This chapter will examine the clinical arena further, after the initial assessment meeting has taken place, thinking about how to develop a therapeutic alliance with a new client and utilizing the concepts of transference and countertransference (see Chapter Three). The clinical framework will be a relational one, drawing from psychoanalytic concepts, such as "holding", and their application to multi-cultural settings. The focus is the exploration of different cultures/realities, and the engagement with our clients, as it is meaningful to them at a particular time and how it influences current psychological issues and the expression of psychological distress.

There are some basic ingredients necessary for any successful therapeutic encounter, such as the concepts of "therapeutic alliance", "containment" and "holding". First and foremost, the therapist begins by nurturing the "therapeutic alliance", or what Erikson (1950) called the "basic trust", referring to the early trust of the infant developed towards the primary care-giver. If the person has been able to "internalize" (or, literally, take something into one's mind as a mental representation) something positive in their early relationship, and has not experienced a high degree of emotional deprivation, then this will be transferred to the therapeutic relationship. However, if a positive relationship has not been internalized, people may find the intimacy and commitment of the therapeutic relationship simply overwhelming. Different theorists have different ideas on the actual "start" of therapy and whether, as Anna Freud (1928) suggested, a "pre-treatment" or "introductory phase" is necessary. Although Anna Freud later dropped this emphasis, it is a concept to be considered in transcultural work when there may not be any trust that people of other races/cultures can (emotionally) bear clients' stories. If trust is allowed to develop, then clients can address more culturally conflicting material.

The concept of "holding" is another essential therapeutic tool, initially introduced by Winnicott (1990), to refer to the intolerable state an infant feels and how he needs both the mother's physical and emotional holding to calm his distress. In the context of parenting, it means that if the parent can manage their own feelings, then the baby can be supported to bear its own anxiety/distress (Kernberg et al., 1972; Zetzel, 1965). This means a sense of tolerating something that feels intolerable for the baby. They are too young and immature to do it for themselves. There is a parallel with therapy, in that if we are able to tolerate the distress and pain of our clients, in turn it might make them feel better equipped to manage these and help them feel they are not falling apart psychically. The concept of holding goes hand in hand with that of "emotional containment", coined by Bion (1962, 1970). Containment implies an ability to take in the material, a bit like a container, to "digest" it mentally and present it back to the person. This takes place either through a verbal comment, or, more subtly, simply through the emotional atmosphere. It implies that there is a communication to the client in way that is manageable for them, and they feel that the therapist is strong enough to hear whatever they need to say. This means that we withstand the material, however painful it is, and, through the naming of the client's feelings/experiences or identifying feelings, the client is made to feel that he or she can bear his or her difficult feelings. An example of this is a client who came back after a very painful disclosure, with great relief that I was still around to listen and that her distress had been named. She said that it felt as if someone was looking after her with a warm blanket.

The paradox here is for the therapist to allow themselves to become emotionally touched by the material, but also to retain a part as our professional thinking space. We strive not to feel the full impact on behalf of the client, but, of course, at times, this is exactly what we feel or the client quite *unconsciously* wishes us to feel. If something is completely alien to us, we simply will not be able to "psychologically travel" there, or even just simply be alongside our clients.

Therapeutic change takes place not only from the relief of our clients in being able to share painful material and understanding, but also the therapist needs to hold on to some hope about the client and have the ability and interest to draw on the client's history. Across many schools of thinking, and within psychoanalysis, there is now more emphasis on the "here and now" and the interpersonal aspects of the therapy. The "here and now" implies a past situation being re-enacted and re-experienced with the aim of eventually losing some intensity, or even acquiring a slightly different meaning. Stern talks about "moments of meeting", referring to therapeutic presence, and if they can really "meet" or connect with the client then it can be a transforming experience. The whole experience of being with a particular other, who will contain and support them, is extremely powerful and emotionally charged. We always seek relationship to others, and we work together with the client to co-construct meaning. Furthermore, Stern states that "language itself could not arise without 'intersubjective relatedness'. You do not talk to someone unless you believe that they can share your mental landscape and act accordingly" (2004, p. 103). It is interesting how much time we spend on understanding intersubjectivity and practising it, particularly at the earlier developmental stages. So, the therapeutic relationship is a unique intersubjective encounter. It is a transitional space created by both therapist and client, in which they can observe the client's current state of mind and anxieties and how they are played out between them. Winnicott (1971) elaborates further that the therapist allows room, or what he calls the "potential space" or capacity, to play. We follow the client's pace, letting things unfold, and, at times, clients need to go over something again and again. Cultural reminiscing may be part of this repetition, considering losses, but also possible gains.

From the outset, we develop what have been called "internal working models", which we continually re-enact. Both the client and therapist can end up re-enacting rich past scenarios and relationships. It is not a re-experiencing process only: in fact, at times, it is a way of helping the client away from retraumatization; a way of gaining a new experience in terms of their history. Although, we expect the client to re-enact relationships and, at times, push this on to the therapist, the therapist is expected to have done sufficient personal development themselves in order not to get caught up in these. For example, feeling like the persecuting father of the client and behaving like it. However, this happens more often than most therapists would care to admit, and often, depending on the severity and therapeutic alliance, there is room for repair, or for the client to go over without experiencing the same previous scenario.

When is the presenting issue about culture?

Clients seek therapy when they feel they have reached a point when they can no longer cope alone with their emotions, and when they need another person to listen and support them. One of therapist's functions is to mirror back to clients their feelings, especially if they feel they do not know what image/person they are projecting in their relationships. The therapist can only empathize in relation to her or his own experience, which may have different socio-cultural referents.

It does not necessarily mean, though, that all clients from different backgrounds will present cross-cultural issues as problematic. Culture is part of their context, and should be addressed as such. When the distress is about cross-cultural issues, the client may indicate this. Often, the more conflict there is about cross-cultural issues, the more likely it is that the issues will be presented in a rather "disguised" form. By disguised, I mean the material is presented in a hidden manner, either because it is out of the client's awareness or because the client is really unsure of how the therapist will react. This perhaps communicates the level of the emotional intensity attached to the material. Being from a minority background, the client may have not had the opportunity to discuss her or his experiences of moving from one culture to another, or of racism, or prejudice. Nevertheless, in my experience with intercultural work, race and cultural issues seem to arise from the first therapy session. It is interesting to note that in therapeutic centres, which are described explicitly as intercultural, clients appear to have more "freedom" to talk about cultural issues or racism, as if they have been permitted to do so. This, in itself, inevitably brings a myriad of other assumptions, and it is just as important to avoid collusion or over-identification with the client (see Akhtar, 2006).

How cultural background, experiences, values, and attitudes influence the psychological process: integrating the inner and outer world

It is useful to begin the clinical work with the client's assumptions of what the therapeutic process entails. If the client is not familiar with the therapy process, it may be necessary to establish their notion of care and support. "Caring" for the client may incorporate their cultural notion of what is appropriate support/care/therapy, who the appropriate "healer" might be, what type of process and length of support is required. It is always vital to find out where the client is in relation to their culture, and how much the client wishes to move out of their cultural framework. This implies the motivation to learn/understand other cultural ways of viewing the world. As Kareem states, cross-cultural therapy "takes into account the whole being of the patient—not only the individual concepts and constructs as presented to the therapist, but also the patient's communal life experience— both past and present" (1992, p. 14).

Following on from this, one hopes that the therapeutic process can contribute to what already is an "improvizational culture" (Myerhoff, 1978). This implies that the culture is made up, as people have different experiences and needs during different life stages, and becomes more creative and fitting with the client's true self.

As stated in an earlier chapter (see Chapter Five), when conducting an assessment with a new client, one has to be careful to take a close enough stance that they are involved with the patient, but at the same time that they are not so close that it prevents a professional stance. I think it is crucial to retain a naturalness in the relationship with the client, and if the therapist has had enough self-development and feels comfortable with her or himself, this will be communicated to the client. I really strongly believe that remaining in too much of a neutral stance can create high levels of anxiety. As Alfille and Cooper remind us, "the most basic ingredient of an attitude of naturalness includes conveying the idea that one is genuinely on the side of the patient" (2002, p. 20). Furthermore, they add that "too much frustration, particularly at the beginning of therapy, can drive someone mad or discourage him from embarking on analytic treatment" (*ibid.*, p. 21), or, indeed, other types of non-intensive therapy. If a client is telling us about something horrendous that has never been validated before, then a human response is necessary. A human response implies respectfulness, although it still implies non self-disclosure and adhering to the therapeutic boundaries (timing, setting, no contact outside meetings, among many other parameters). There is always careful observation of what route they might take in their narrative, body posture, or emotional state before sharing any comments with the client. Furthermore, having the appropriate "distance" implies that the professional can still retain a professional thinking hat and experience the client without reaching conclusions prematurely or inappropriately.

So far, all the issues mentioned are general issues that apply to any client; however, there are some specific issues when working with someone from a different cultural background. One of the aims of clinical work is towards integration of internal, psychological conflicts, as well as culturally conflicting elements. Adams (1996) discusses psychical integration as a way of acknowledging the different parts of a person, and recognition that they are different and will remain so. This is the fine line in therapeutic work, to address the inner world of the client, but, at the same time, keep a space for the external, interpersonal, and cultural influences and the personal meaning they hold. This also means keeping a space for not knowing, letting the client surprise us with their journey. Emotionally, this is sometimes a really difficult place to be, but an essential ingredient of psychotherapeutic work. If either route is followed, only the intrapsychic or the cultural, it is unhelpful, as the cultural creates and intensifies stereotypes and the purely intrapsychic stance means we do not see the person in their cultural context.

The therapist can validate the client's experience and identity. Clients are often concerned about relaying something, in case it is not heard, is minimized, or altered in meaning. If the person who has the authority (even if we do not like to think of ourselves in this way, our clients come to us in distress, so it is not an equal relationship from the outset), such as the therapist, provides the validation, then this creates a kind of emotional healing for the client. Even if their external circumstances do not necessarily change, their perception might have altered significantly). If it is properly "heard" through the meeting of the two people, then it will create emotional relief. There are significant moments of relief during the course of the therapy that we should keep close attention as to when they take place.

Clinical vignettes

The following case material illustrates the themes and the challenges faced in therapeutic work. As there is not one homogeneous community or culture, a clinical vignette will serve to illustrate specific dynamics of cross-cultural work with a particular person within a particular relationship.

Alessandro

Alessandro, a thirty-year-old man, came to see me after taking time off work for ill health. When I asked him about his background, he looked extremely surprised and described himself rather uncomfortably as coming from "mixed parentage". His mother was British and his father was originally from Africa and had settled in Brazil. Alessandro was brought up in South America, where his parents had met and lived together in Brazil until he was five years old. He had then moved with his mother to the USA, and remained there until he was twenty-two years old. Alessandro had come over to the UK to study, but later, as he said rather passively, "just ended up staying", as many immigrants do, for another year and then another, which ended up being eight years in total. He has been in a series of short-term relationships, and after the last relationship broke up he felt utterly hopeless that he could maintain anything long-term. He had been prescribed antidepressants by his doctor, and he had reluctantly agreed. He told me that it had made him feel even more of a failure for not coping, and that he was finding it hard to hold on to any motivation in his life. For example, there were many decisions that had been abandoned for some time, such as his returning to work. I met a man whom I can only describe as "lost" in every way, personally, socially, and professionally. His tone was flat and hollow.

Initially, although he had requested to work with someone from another culture to himself, he did not really think it was important to discuss this. In fact, I was interested in what words he used to define his culture (his English was fluent, but he still thought in Spanish). He found this so difficult to do, and said he had never really had the space to think about it. Unconsciously, he related to me as if I was the key to the British culture, commented on how good my English was (by saying this, of course he was acknowledging that I was also from another culture). If he visited a new place in Britain, he would assume I had been there, and, if not, that "I knew all about it". It was as if I was the one who had completely embraced the host culture, very much as he had tried to do for the time he had been in the UK. When his relationship with a British woman had finished, he had to review his life. One aspect that he considered is that in his relationships, he sought to be with women who were also slightly "lost" culturally. His last relationship epitomized this, where he chose to be with someone who worked for the Red Cross and frequently travelled abroad at short notice and felt rather an outsider in her own culture. During those times, he described how difficult it had been for him to hold on to any continuity in their relationship. He realized that there was an element in him that he had not quite acknowledged and, therefore, unconsciously, he chose people who were similar and slightly nomadic, and, sadly, emotionally uncommitted. In a way, he did not know how to keep a relationship, especially a cross-cultural one, as he had never had a model of this. Now we were in a transcultural therapeutic relationship and it was a good starting point, but I had to be on guard as his non-committal part was finding it hard to attend regularly, on time, and I had to find a way to contain him and keep timings regular.

I slowly understood how much he wanted to fit in and have a home. Back "home" in the USA, he felt torn between his father's culture and race and his mother's. When he felt safe enough to discuss his childhood and family relationships, I learnt that the parental relationship had been looked down upon by his maternal grandparents, and in fact there had not been much contact with them. He realized how furious he was that he knew so little about his mother's background and that she had never really introduced him to her family. He felt she had found a refuge in another country, just like his own reasons for coming to the UK. Most of his contact had been with his father's relatives, but that stopped a few years after his parents separated. He had taken on board the parental values placed on race and culture to such an extent that it became impossible to feel that he could be himself—that is, a man of mixed parentage.

For many people of mixed parentage, when the parents are seen not to be able to hold the diversity there is no model for the young person for how to engage in their most intimate relationships. Alessandro attempted to do this by being in his own "neutral ground", as he called it, although, of course, he had returned to his mother's home culture. Initially, being in London made him feel very different and he was desperate to fit in. But later, he began to like the fact that London was multi-cultural and enjoyed not being placed into a slot automatically. In the beginning of the therapy, one of the obstacles had been that he wanted to travel, but he postponed obtaining a new passport. This was due to his wish to change his surname and take on his mother's British name. He later gave up this wish and said it meant that he could hold on to his identity and not have to fulfil her wish to belong. Like so many clients, he felt he was not only seen as, but that inside he felt more, "Spanish" in Britain, while he was seen and felt as more British in South America, and as "black" in the USA. This is quite common, where people hold on to more than one identity, determined by the different environments (Thomas & Schwarzbaum, 2006).

At first, Alessandro needed to put aside our cultural differences and see me as fitting into the British culture completely. It was too painful for him not to belong, so he had to feel I had managed it. Of course, this pretence could not last as he began to be in touch with the emotional cost of fitting in and rejecting his diverse background. Also, it was impossible to do, as he was constantly asked about his origin. At a later stage, he asked me whether I was also of "mixed" background. In his eyes, this meant we could understand each other. He felt it enabled us to work with his material, and at times I think he hoped, because of the commonalities (from his perspective), we would not have to cover certain areas which were best left uncovered. During this phase of the transcultural therapy, he seemed to make observations of objects in the consulting room that he assumed I had obtained from abroad. I reflected this back to him, and how he had let go of the image of me as belonging to the majority culture. We linked it with the parallel in his life where, rather than "fitting in"; it became more meaningful to him to integrate all the cultural components of his diverse background.

I have chosen this clinical case because it illustrates many poignant cross-cultural themes discussed earlier. In this case, we had to address both the similarities and the differences between us, and both of us being part of a different context. As stated earlier, each culture has a different view of the developmental stages and the goals expected at each stage. In Alessandro's case, he was approaching thirty and was struggling with his own cultural expectations as well as the majority culture expectations of what he "ought to be doing with his life". To his surprise, many of the internally imposed expectations were in line with Spanish cultural expectations. The case also illustrates that the experience of "culture shock" (Littlewood & Lipsedge, 1989), which includes the sadness, fear, and anger about being in a different context, is not necessarily triggered on entry to the new culture and it does not always have to be a negative experience. For Alessandro, coming to Britain had been a turbulent journey, but it was not explored until some years later. Once he entered the exploration process, he felt there was so much that had been pushed aside, and it was time to review his identity and be proud of his roots.

It is interesting that when asked about significant attachments in the beginning, he had said humorously about a potential therapist that "it didn't matter who they were as long as they liked South Americans and they did not think they all were into drugs". It was a revelation to him how he had devalued himself to such an extent and was fearful of being judged (but, of course, not to undermine how external stereotypes fuelled his own feelings). Clients often will bring stereotypical images before the therapist does so, as this is part of their experience through societal images. It was brought into our consulting room as a way of testing any stereotypes I might hold. It was my responsibility to open it up for exploration with him. Emotionally, Alessandro was at a stage of his life where he was open to change. Since he had grown up multi-culturally, he was also more at ease at being in a transcultural therapeutic relationship, and I have no doubt that from the very beginning he sensed my own ease with cross-cultural travels.

Andrea

Andrea, a Greek-Cypriot client, in her mid-fifties, was referred for therapy after repeated visits to her new Greek doctor. Her doctor, being British-educated, believed that the client was suffering from depression and needed help, so he referred her to a psychiatrist. She attended for two sessions, and then wished to stop, although she complied with the prescribed medication for depression. The other diagnosis that was identified was obsessive compulsive disorder (OCD). The psychiatrist suggested a referral to a Greek-speaking therapist, and she came to me a few months later. She explained that she has been suffering for years, but she could not confide this to anyone who was "foreign". The reason for this was that her spoken English was poor, and she would rarely mix with anyone non-Greek. She was able to speak to the Greek doctor because a male doctor in her culture holds high status. She responded readily to my enquiry about her thoughts regarding the therapy, saying that it was her first experience of direct help. She had strong doubts as to whether talking alone would alleviate her problems, but she agreed to attend to please her doctor and her family (who made her promise to them that she would at least attend the first few sessions).

I was faced with unravelling the personal and cultural components of the depression and the OCD. First of all, the "depression" seemed more like fury and shame, linked to her daughter's new relationship with a mixed-race man. Although she had hoped it would stop, she saw that she was serious about the relationship for the first time, and they were expecting a child together. She was overwhelmed with concern about what other people in the community would think. She was painfully aware of how much she had wished she could "marry her off", especially to another Greek boy, as she was over forty, but disappointed about "the way things had turned out". Her daughter also lived at home, which was seen as problematic by the doctor. In some cultures, children are encouraged to stay closer to the parents or the primary care-giver than in others, and it continues throughout adulthood (for further cultural examples, see Kakar, 1981).

In terms of the OCD issue, I was very aware that Andrea had a high level of anxiety around cleanliness, and her fears of infection were preoccupying her thinking, but that there were cultural ideas on cleanliness that I had to take into account. It is not unusual to meet a Greek woman of her age who does not allow any pet in the house, has to cover the furniture, washes vegetables in the sink with soap, etc. So, I worked on what would be negotiable for her and what would be unacceptable to her culturally. She believed that there had already been a "cathartic" effect (or relief) by breaking her silence, and so we met regularly for a brief period of time. Therapy was experienced as "companionship" (her words in Greek), which took place once a week. She wanted to return the "favour" of my attentiveness and listening, and invite me to her home to offer me "a coffee and a sweet", which is a common gesture of hospitality in a Greek Cypriot household. Although I declined, I had to find the right words to address this without sounding rejecting. This is a regular event with Greek-Cypriot clients, especially first generation immigrants. She told me that she was so grateful that she could not imagine not giving me anything back. Letting go of cultural ideas and ignoring others' comments about her daughter was difficult for her, but she appreciated the freedom to discuss it with another Greek person.

Nick

A thirty-year-old man, Nick, came to see me after many years of suffering from "mental health problems", clinical depression, and suicidal feelings. He had been on antidepressant medication for many years. He was referred by his key worker after his own request that "he needed someone to talk to who would understand" what kind of person he really was. He had seen other professionals briefly, but had never had any long-term continuity with a professional apart from a psychiatrist.

In the first session, he was extremely nervous and fidgety. He told me about his psychiatrist, who was a Sri Lankan man described as a "quiet old man". Nick had felt he could not "fault" him, as he had "put up" with him and his moaning over the years, but implied that he really did not know what to do with him. I wondered whether there were some links with the father here, who would see him sporadically, and there were crises that he could not possibly begin to tell him. He also felt that because we all "put up with him", he had to somehow be grateful and not be angry with us for the amount of times he felt lonely and alone and we were not there to take away these feelings. My initial feeling was to want to be the "better parent" for him, but I knew that I had to work hard not to occupy that role, as I would only fail. He had had so many losses, and his internal world expected people to leave him. His mother died prior to his fifth birthday, and so he had multiple and broken attachments since. I had to allow an "unconscious free-floating responsiveness" (Sandler, Dare & Holder, 1992), or a sort of countertransference, where we are drawn to the client's inner world and we behave like people from their past. Of course, as therapists, we need to keep thinking about our responses in supervision and use anything that feels odd or puzzling as an insight into their world.

Nick brought a bag of documents to each session, which he wanted me to read, but somehow there was never the time, so we could never sift through it all. In fact, as I learnt subsequently, it was to be an ongoing theme; Nick's bag was almost like a "this is your life book". It contained a copy of his birth certificate, and childhood pictures. He carried them with him to most places, as if they were a reminder of who he was, where he belonged, and, to some extent, what he wanted to find out about himself: the bag contained all the information, as if he could compensate for the missing years, which were reflected in the missing pictures, documents, etc. Sadly, it also reflected how he felt that he was in "pieces". Initially, he referred to his key worker as the "white woman" and me as the person who, in his words, was "black and different". He idealized this relationship with me, as the first person that he felt comfortable being with. He found it hard to come on time, and we would regularly miss large chunks of the session. My gut feeling would be to "worry" about something dreadful having happened to him. He contributed to this, by his tone sometimes of telling me things to worry about and then saying "but don't worry, I wouldn't do it". He would then turn up in the following session and say that something dreadful had happened. In fact, the dreadful thing came from within, rather than external events. He would talk about events, however, as if they had happened only that week. A recurring story was the betrayal of his father. He would drop by to see him, and he would be too busy. Nick would then proceed to go on to stories of many years ago as if it had happened that week. It would be so impossible to distinguish between what was current and what was an event from years ago. All memory is reconstructed, to an extent, but in this case, it would be rather confusing. The most important thing with him was to "tell his story", which was so bottled up. He would talk incessantly without gaps, constantly looking at the clock despairingly, being in touch with "how little time there was". As I would say it was time to end the session, his face would be like an abandoned boy, filled with sadness and bewilderment. It had a similar quality to the boy called "John" in the Robertsons' video (Robertson & Robertson, 1989), who was left in the care of nurses while his mother was in hospital.

One day, when he was looking at the clock, I said that it also felt as if there was very little time for us. It put him in touch with how he had felt angry about his mother's death and the fact that it came out of the blue, without warning, he said. She had a car accident while visiting her family in South America. He felt this was a cruel experience for a young boy to have to go through. He said it was as if they reclaimed her and she no longer was torn, but what about all of us left behind? Every event after this meant no preparation and no security. He had spend most of his life thinking "what if" and almost leading a double life, imagining what it would have been like had his mother lived. It was important that he mourned for her and, of course, this is an experience that would never be erased, but he had not been able to think of a future. Mourning enabled him to own some feelings that had been far too painful to hold on to and he had often powerfully passed them on to me.

Often, it is worth waiting before making any significant interpretations with clients who had not had a significant attachment. Similarly with Nick, I had to work hard to establish basic relating and attunement (a deeply emotional connection), which he had only experienced in his very early life. I had to also make sure I was realistic about what he could take in and I was aware of the "pain of contrast" (Casement, 1999, pp. 106–107; 2006), or his realization of what he never had and how painful it would be to be in touch with his losses and how much parenting he had not had. Once I felt there was a bit more connection, then we could go on to a stage of sameness, and then on to a differentiation phase. Interestingly for him, this came abruptly one day when he looked at me and said suddenly that I looked like a judge in a room; he did not label me as "white", but I knew it had triggered experiences when he had to stand in front of a white judge, who would "judge him whatever he said because he was black". Interestingly, although I had to withstand a great deal of aggression from him (just as he had been bullied, it was now felt to be directed from me and, of course, at times, I would experience it as coming from him), I knew something had shifted as he stopped carrying as many belongings around with him. Instead, he just carried a smaller load, still needed, a bit like his transitional object, but he was beginning to experience himself in his skin/psyche as having less "leaks". In other words, he could somehow feel he was more contained in both his mind and his body as a result of feeling more contained through the transcultural therapy work. In conclusion, it felt as if "he was able to emerge from the psychic retreat to make contact with the psychic reality he may be able to recognize sufficient good feelings to enable him to feel regret and remorse" (Steiner, 1993, p. xiii).

External links

For some clients who find that they feel hopelessness, we have to find a way to mobilize their inner resources, as well as any cultural rituals or support that might be of comfort. In practice, it can be much more effective when the local cultural support is accessed alongside the therapy. For other clients, it may actually be a time that they, themselves, seek to be away from cultural groups, because that is where the problem lies, or there is shame about the issues. So, although this does not work for all clients, it is an area we can explore and then let the client decide whether it would be useful. If the resources are available, there are also times when it might be useful to set up support resources, such as a therapy group for mothers, or adolescents with similar issues.

When I worked as a staff counsellor at one of the London hospitals, I joined a psychology colleague to co-run a monthly support group for Bangladeshi interpreters. The women were consulted on what would be helpful for them, the frequency of the meetings they required, and it was agreed that the group would be held in English. On special occasions, they brought food from their country to share (after some discussion, since this group had therapeutic elements, but it was not strictly a therapeutic group, bringing along food was thought to be appropriate and aided in bonding with their peers). As the women were feeling rather unappreciated in their work setting, the group provided the opportunity to integrate some of the powerful emotional stories with each other, and digest how much they had to carry for their clients. If they were contained, then their clients could be contained, but also the group was a forum of having a space to understand their involvement and to try to maintain professional boundaries.

Issues of gender/race and cultural/religious over-identification could be thought about in depth, so their interventions remained as objective and client-centred as possible. The majority of these women had felt rather isolated socially and did not have the traditional support they would have had back home, so there was a great relief in belonging to a women's group. As one woman said to me, 'If I was to have a family, I can't imagine not having my mother around to support me; this is like my adopted family in the UK.'

Dreams

Dreams hold different meanings for different cultural groups. In psychoanalytic psychotherapy, dreams often hold the hidden (out-of-awareness) treasure of the psyche. They provide this hidden information about the client's internal conflicts and cross-cultural issues. I emphasize the importance of dreams and explicitly ask clients to try to remember dreams, especially if they are new to psychotherapy. This way, it already gives them a different kind of importance, even if, consciously, people think they do not remember their dreams. We are all immersed in a subjective experience and we have to hear what meanings the dream has which are unique to the dreamer, represented in images and words. When they bring a dream, I ask them to recall it without trying to put connections (most people do this anyway). It is a way of not losing hold of the dream's unconscious content. Then I ask them to repeat it, as if they are going through it again in that present moment. Most people do not think they can remember more, and yet, every time they go through it, they are surprised how much more they can remember. It seems to trigger their memory and more information about the dream emerges, such as whether they were facing the person or they were turning away, issues of distance between people, what they saw while doing something else, etc. As Freud (1900a) said, they are "the royal road to the unconscious", and certainly they also open the door to other meaningful experiences that are embedded in a particular racial and cultural context.

There is very little writing on dreams and their relationship to racial and cultural components. There are many clinical literature examples where dreams, objects, and people change and merge, but very little on how nationalities can alter and there is completely fluidity as to how they change. Adams (1996) is one of the few writers who provide vivid examples of people's changing racial characteristics during dreaming. It alerts us to enquire more about the racial and cultural aspects of dreams, as they are often left out of the conscious mind. If one becomes open to these issues, it is not unusual to find out from a client that in their dream the therapist has taken on their culture, or even race, and vice versa. This puts the therapist in rather new territory as someone of a different race/culture. Related to this, it is interesting to note that often pregnant women (who are already experiencing vivid dreams due to their profound hormonal changes and also psychological experience) talk about fears that their baby will turn into another culture or race (or fulfilling their wish that the baby will belong to a different race or culture). The meanings of this may be quite different, depending on the dreamer. For one client, who had been adopted, it represented a feeling connected to her own sense of racial/cultural loss and a wish to have some sense of belongingness, and for another it was a feeling about losing her baby to her family, a value system that she felt she did not adhere to, but she was aware that it felt like a battleground since her pregnancy.

Kathy

An Irish client whom I had been working with produced a very interesting dream one day. The dream was following a session cancellation on my part, due to illness.

The dream:

> I was walking somewhere around a hospital, when I saw an elderly woman sitting down near a fountain. She looked troubled, but I had to rush past her as I was in a hurry. . . . I can't really remember any more of the dream.

It is not unusual that clients cannot remember the whole dream from the onset. Dreams represent the incoherent part of the mind that processes our experiences and affect. They store material from the past and present experiences, but not in any historical order. Hence, dreams can be a mixture of events that seem extremely muddled and meaningless. It is important to persevere with meanings and revisit in subsequent sessions if appropriate, as they hold significant information. I usually let clients just talk about dreams the first time round, without any interruption, and then I ask them to go back into it as if they were in the present. Again, they may say that they do not remember much, but most times further details emerge and, in turn, they trigger further material. With Kathy, when she went back into the dream, she described this woman as "traditional, you know, with a headscarf". Later she remembered that she was Turkish (said with uncertainty). Another bit of information was that she remembered the colour of her eyes. At this point I listened, observing how she was speaking from the unconscious. Then there was a pause . . . and she thought they looked a bit like mine. Then she smiled. As there was some conscious realization her posture changed, became rather fidgety, and shifted position slightly away from me. I was aware of this, as I found myself shifting to face the client and realized I was responding to something she was communicating. Then she seemed deep in thought and I felt she was distant. At this point, I wondered how the dream had left her in the morning. She said it had left her feeling concerned about this woman, but she was "only human after all", and, in a rather irritated manner, that she was "a nurse, but could not look after everybody, so it was just as well that she wanted to see a female professional". So, this was the new piece of information, that the elderly woman insisted on seeing a female nurse. This was a common occurrence in the hospital, but interesting to unravel the meaning in my client's dream.

Making interpretations, especially with racial, cultural content, one has to tread very carefully, particularly when those interpretations are of an ethnic racial nature. It is always revealing to discover where the clients' dreams take place; in the new environment, or in the old environment, and how integrated are the two settings? If they are integrated, how do they come together? There are so many layers of reality, racial and cultural dynamics, and, of course, the individual meanings. I had worked with Kathy long enough, however, to know that she was someone who knew well the political history between Greeks and Turks and had always identified with the Greek-Cypriots. After all, she also was aware of some of the stereotypes inflicted on her as an Irishwoman. I was aware that I was seeing this client in a hospital setting, and was struck by this rich communication. Also, we were working in an area where ethnic minorities from Greek and Turkish backgrounds were predominant. She added an interesting dimension in that I was experienced as an elderly woman, perhaps like her own elderly mother. Her mother had never had the time for her, but in the dream she was the one that did not have time for this woman, just as I had not had the time for her the previous week, when I had to cancel our meeting. Furthermore, I was made into someone not only of another ethnicity, but someone who was seen as an aggressor (historically) by Greeks. This process enabled me to challenge her and to open up the whole area of her identification with the Greeks. We explored the common ground she had with them, but how she was also different from them. This brought out a significant and painful aspect of her. In fact, she identified to a high degree with this North London Greek family, which had become almost like a surrogate family for her. We had explored this at length, in terms of her wish to distance herself from her difficult family as well as the ethnic Irish stereotypes. She had even talked about wishing to learn Greek one day. Boyd-Franklin (1989) discusses the formation of "fictive kin", which is a chosen family, created when people find themselves abroad.

Kathy's dream presented many rich meanings and layers. She had recently visited her mother in Ireland and had wanted to tell her about her sexuality, but felt with her mother's ill health, she would never understand and once again left Ireland, choosing to "take the secret", as she called it, back with her (a place that was very familiar for her, as she had spent a childhood of secrets). In her dream, the elderly Turkish woman did not wish to see her, but another nurse. She had always sensed that she reminded her mother of her estranged father, who had physically abused her and her mother for years. Needless to say, she was revealing her deep fear that I would also not accept her sexuality, just like her mother, and also her new-found Greek family. In fact, she had mentioned it to her Greek friends, and had sat through many jokes about potential marriages to Greek men. There is much more material to analyse in this case than the dream material, but the intention of this case vignette was to show the reader how the external and internal once again are so intertwined. You can also see that had I not addressed these dynamics, the therapy could not have reached some of the more difficult and ambivalent layers of the psyche. This case was chosen for discussion, as it is representative of a particular relationship, in a particular cultural and racial context. In the countertransference, I had to tolerate numerous projections, including emotive racial and cultural stereotypes.

Endings

Endings are difficult for any client, and we need to take time to prepare our clients and to make sure that this is what they truly wish to do. An adequate time for goodbyes depends on their issues and how long we have been working together. The ending stage can be the most stressful for many clients (Mishne, 2002). If there is the luxury of unlimited time, then the concluding phase can be paced, in order to ensure that all of the issues have been worked through properly. However, due to long waiting lists and economic pushes favouring short-term models, many services dictate shorter term treatment, which raises ethical and clinical questions for therapists. However, even if the work is short-term, it is imperative that the client is informed as soon as possible so that they can have some control, they can have sufficient grieving time and think about the optimum future direction. This especially applies to clients with a history of loss and separation trauma. Premature ending can leave a client feeling a sense of abandonment and disillusionment (Mishne, 2002): that is, just as they have begun to trust someone and disclose their distress, it gets taken away. For clients who come from familial or cultural backgrounds that discourage openly exhibiting anger or disappointment, it is therapeutic to leave time to work through this, but gently, in order that the client is not left feeling guilty for confronting the authority figure.

For any client, but particularly those who are already cautious about mainstream services, it may mean that we never really get to know the full extent of their distress. During the ending phase, previous losses and endings will be re-evoked. For the cross-culturally different client who has migrated, endings will be emotionally loaded with memories of those they long to see, or, for the refugee, those that remain out of their reach as they cannot travel or they are still missing. If there was mistrust about attending in the first place, then one hopes their view has changed. One hopes that there has been enough time to rework life issues, have a sense of a greater self unity and integration, and renewed hope for new life and relationship opportunities.

In conclusion, the therapist has been discussed as someone who has the training and personal analysis to equip her with a particular space for others' distress, and who has the mental space for the whole of the person. This means to view them within their family, their culture, and race, and all that they may have taken on consciously and unconsciously about their culture. Containment, or attunement to our clients, means that we listen carefully for the cultural cues, conscious and unconscious messages, body language, and relating that are all essential if we are to really engage and support them. The concepts of transference and countertransference are extremely useful in a cross-cultural therapeutic encounter, and, of course, the therapist, just like the client, brings expectations, hopes, and repetitions of their history with the client. We need to distinguish what might be a cultural or racial transference and not necessarily stemming only from the parents. As shown by the clinical examples, what goes on out there in society inevitably filters into the consulting room.

Clients can feel *heard and cared for* if the emotional atmosphere and their material (experiences conveyed) is endured. Similar to the

previous chapter, we have to keep in mind the individual's uniqueness and personality interacting with the family, as well as being
within a particular culture as a triad model of psycho-social
influences from the beginning. Another ingredient is to let the client
be the "driver" in terms of the route they take, personally or in
terms of their relationship to cultural and racial elements. The
central issue in transcultural work is *how* to take on board race and
culture in the consultation room, without making it the central
issue. Additionally, it is crucial not to get caught up in matching the
therapist and client dyad purely on racial and cultural factors and
to feel sufficiently comfortable to challenge racial and cultural
issues, should they arise. Obviously, the focus here has been cross-
cultural issues, but there are other factors such as the therapist's
age, gender, and style, which will affect the therapy. However, I
strongly believe that the therapeutic relationship tends to break
down right in the beginning if cross-cultural issues are not
addressed. Finally, I would like to end with Greenson's statement
that the therapist "must safeguard the patient's self-respect and
sense of dignity" (1985, p. 378). In order to do so, we must be aware
that our therapeutic frame is a very useful one, but not one, we can
hide behind, as our views and values sometimes are more trans-
parent than what we think.

References

Adams, M. V. (1996). *Multicultural Imagination: "Race", Colour, and the
    Unconscious*. London: Routledge.
Akhtar, S. (2006). Technical challenges faced by the immigrant psycho-
    analyst. *Psychoanalytic Quarterly, 75*: 21–43.
Alfille, H., & Cooper, J. (2002). *Dilemmas in the Consulting Room*.
    London: Karnac.
Bion, W. (1962). *Learning from Experience*. London: Heinemann.
Bion, W. (1970). *Attention and Interpretation*. London: Tavistock.
Boyd-Franklin, N. (1989). *Black Families in Therapy: A Multisystems
    Approach*. New York: Guilford Press.
Casement, P. (1990). *Further Learning—The Patient: The Analytic Space
    and Process*. London: Routledge.
Casement, P. (2006). *Learning from Life: Becoming a Psychoanalyst*.
    London: Routledge.

Erikson, E. (1950). *Childhood and Society*. New York: W. W. Norton.

Freud, A. (1928). *Introduction to the Technique of Child Analysis*. New York/Washington: Nervous and Mental Disease Publishing.

Freud, S. (1900a). *The Interpretation of Dreams*. *S.E.*, 4–5. London: Hogarth.

Greenson, R. (1985). *The Technique and Practice of Psycho-Analysis*. London: Hogarth Press/Institute of Psychoanalysis.

Kakar, S. (1981). *The Inner World*. Delhi: Oxford University Press.

Kareem, J. (1992). The Nafsiyat intercultural therapy centre. In: J. Kareem & R. Littlewood (Eds.), *Intercultural Therapy* (pp. 14–37). London: Blackwell.

Kernberg, O., Burnstein, E. D., Coyne, L., Appelbaum, A., Horowitz, L., & Voth, H. (1972). Psychotherapy and psychoanalysis: final part of the Menninger Foundation's Psychotherapy Research Project. *Bulletin of the Menninger Clinic, 36*: 1–275.

Littlewood, R., & Lipsedge, M. (1989). *Intercultural Therapy*. London: Unwin Hyman.

Mishne, J. (2002). *Multiculturalism and the Therapeutic Process*. London: Guilford Press.

Myerhoff, B. (1978). *Number Our Days*. New York: Simon and Schuster.

Robertson, J., & Robertson, J. (1989). *Separation and the Very Young*. London: Free Association Books.

Sandler, J., Dare, C., & Holder, A. (1992). *The Patient and the Analyst*. London: Karnac.

Steiner, J. (1993). *Psychic Retreats*. London: Routledge.

Stern, D. (2004). *The Present Moment in Psychotherapy and Everyday Life*. London: Norton.

Thomas, A. J., & Schwarzbaum, S. (2006). *Culture and Identity*. London: Sage.

Winnicott, D. (1971). *Playing and Reality*. London: Routledge.

Winnicott, D. W. (1990). *The Maturational Processes and the Facilitating Environment*. London: Institute of Psychoanalysis/Karnac.

Zetzel, E. (1965). The theory of therapy in relation to a developmental model of the psychic apparatus. *International Journal of Psycho-analysis, 46*: 39–52.

CHAPTER SEVEN

The psycho-social experiences of different immigrant groups and the multi-faceted migration journey

Zack Eleftheriadou

The first aim of this chapter is to outline the psycho-social experiences of different immigrant groups. It is not intended to create or reinforce stereotypes about particular groups, but rather to educate the therapist on the reality and difference of the client's external world. The second aim is to examine what it means to move from one cultural context to another. The whole psychological journey, from the point of thinking of moving to the actual move and the whole "settling experience" will be explored, using clinical case material and drawing from non-clinical populations' written accounts. People demonstrate vast differences in their capacity to be in a new cultural environment.

An overview of the multi-cultural population of Britain

Currently, the predominant minority ethnic groups in the UK come from India, Pakistan, the West Indies, Africa, Cyprus, and Turkey, and more recently, Eastern European countries such as the Czech Republic, Slovakia, Poland, Bulgaria, and Romania. These populations share commonalities in that they are often seen to be "different"; "foreign", and they are even labelled as being "alien". Although they are perceived to be rather different from the majority population, they have just as many differences between and within them as they do when compared with the majority population, particularly in terms of languages and religions.

Visible and invisible minorities

In the UK, minority groups tend to be divided and, in fact, at times divide themselves, into the "internal immigrants", for example, those who originally come from Scotland, Wales, and Ireland; "white ethnics", including immigrants from North America and European countries. Some European Jewish groups were also minority groups before they came to settle in the UK. The grouping "ethnic minorities" includes immigrants who come from previous Commonwealth countries, such as the West Indies and Cyprus, and the term usually is applied to those of "colour".

In UK society, the different ethnic groups tend to be divided purely on racial characteristics, despite the fact that race itself is no longer viewed as a scientifically valid concept (see Chapters Two and Eleven for more extensive discussion). There is evidence to indicate that those who are from "visible" minority backgrounds have a more difficult time settling in the new environment than religious and other white ethnic minorities, as they tend to remain more "invisible", for example, those of Jewish origin, especially if they have taken on the culture's behaviours, language, and mannerisms. When there are noticeable differences, ethnic minorities often prefer to keep them secret in order not to intensify racism or to be labelled as "defective". For example, Greeks and Greek Cypriots, Turks, Chinese, Bangladeshi, and West Indians, among others, do not openly talk about the hereditary sickle cell anaemia or thalassaemia trait. As a result, it has been rather difficult to provide formal therapeutic support, although this is not to say that these ethnic groups would not use a therapy service (see Eleftheriadou, 1995 for discussion of psycho-social aspects).

The social reality for ethnic minorities

Many ethnic minority groups experience deprivation in terms of housing, education, employment, and health care. Also, as discussed earlier, ethnic minorities, especially those of black origin, are over-represented in the psychiatric services due to racism, oppression, and a genuine lack of understanding of their cultural and individual needs.

By examining a person's socio-cultural context, one allows the person to discover the meaningful elements from their social environment. This is something that emerges from the first therapy meeting (see Chapter Five). At times, they have been described as leading a double life, with one life in the new country and one life back home that they keep in touch with. It is common that if there is an upheaval in terms of socio-political events in their home country, this would preoccupy them during therapy sessions, especially if there are significant events like political elections or the occurrence of a natural disaster.

Common psychological issues

Sense of self before moving and reasons for moving to another culture

People now have the ability to move freely around the world. We are witnessing whole families moving and it has become such a common event that it is important we do not underestimate its unique stresses and pressures (see Akhtar, 1999). There are obvious differences when one chooses to move than when there is forced separation from one's home owing to political and ideological reasons or natural disasters. Migrants have different reasons for moving to another country.

It is important to bear in mind that some of these reasons do not unfold until they have moved to the new environment. For example, some people feel that they have always been the "odd one out" of their family, or they have to deal with many internal problems which seem so overwhelming that the person places more importance on the change of environment in order to overcome them.

Therefore, the person has left in order to seek something "better", to learn more, provide more happiness, money, etc. (or, at least, that is the perception), or in order to escape from something that feels rather persecutory. They equate moving with a new start and a hope that all will change. The new country is looked upon as full of potential and hope. Of course, both the wish to find something better and escaping something can be seen to have positive and negative qualities, depending on how a person has made sense of them. Broadly speaking, there are those people who seek adventure and sometimes risk, who want to visit new places, and those who need many familiar people around them. Everyone has a different capacity to be alone (Winnicott, 1958), but how much one veers away from one's environment is also defined in a familial and cultural way. Winnicott (1971), throughout his book *Playing and Reality*, discusses the notion of "potential space", or the space between the ego and the non-ego and the need to create this. In a sense, the move can require a sudden need for reorganization, and some personality types are more "resilient" than others and cope well.

Primary stress and dislocation

There are many myths about migration (Grinberg & Grinberg, 1989) and there remains the debate as to whether migration is a trauma or not. In this context, it is believed that it is a complex experience that can have negative aspects and positive ones. This is the reason that this chapter contains both clinical vignettes and accounts from non-clinical populations, in order to convey the complexity of this experience. For the refugee or asylum seeker, there will be a different social experience, and, hence, these issues will be discussed in more depth later in the book.

The trauma or distress of moving is experienced over a longer period of time, created by multiple factors. Because it is not observable, it may be difficult to think about and understand. The whole experience and process of migration depends on the individual personality and its resilience (see Akhtar, 1999). There are different ways to deal with migration, some of which we would call more adaptive than others. Others have described the experience like a microscope, which magnifies positive and negative personality traits, such as loneliness and inadequacy. But moving cultures is not all negative; there are undoubtedly positive aspects, for example, that people are exposed to situations and opportunities that they may not have had before. As Mukherjee states,

> The expatriate is the ultimate self-made artist, even the chooser of a language in which to operate . . . It is possible, in expatriation, to step out of the constraints into which one has been born and to exercise to the fullest the dual version of the detached outsider. [1999, p. 72]

There are numerous myths that have tried to explore the themes of moving, such as the "Tower of Babel" myth, where there is desire to "reach heaven" or the ideal, or the Jules Verne (2005) book, *Around the World in Eighty Days*, which is a voyage of curiosity and discovery of things that are almost forbidden. The feelings of those who wish to move on are mixed: sadness, anxiety, and nostalgia, which is sometimes exaggerated, but also expectations and hopes to know more and have new experiences. The confusion can sometimes be experienced as a punishment for wanting to know more, as those who leave can often experience guilt for wanting more than the "mother culture" can offer.

"Cultural inheritance" (Winnicott, 1971) is necessary to ensure continuity of existence. Cultural inheritance is the "potential space" between the individual and the environment (as discussed in the previous chapter in more depth). The person makes sense of this space according to the notion of "me" and "not-me", being within the group of origin and an outside group. Migrants need to develop "potential space" between the lost mother country and the new one, in a similar way to a child needing to play, exploring and creating a link between the self and the environment. If there is a validating environment, then it can support the individual. For the immigrant, it is also a process of gaining new self skills and exploring and developing a new internal and external relationship with the new culture. If this becomes difficult, the person may end up experiencing distress and isolation. The separation from one's culture can be compared to the loss of the "containing object" (Bion, 1970), or the space to feel they are safe and understood, which can make people feel that there will never be a sense of "wholeness" again. There may be strivings to create a new family and ancestors in the new environment.

The acculturation process

Acculturation refers to "the changes that an individual experiences as a result of being in contact with other cultures and as a result of participating in the process of acculturation that his cultural or ethnic group is undergoing" (Berry, Poortinga, Segall, & Dasen, 1992, pp. 271–272). It is the experience of cognitive adjustment (how others think or conceptualize), behavioural adjustment (how others behave and the reasons for particular gestures, rituals, etc.), and emotional (how, when, to what degree, and with whom is it appropriate to express emotionality) adjustment into a new culture. It requires the learning of new skills.

When a new culture is encountered, there is often what has been termed "culture shock". A whole set of completely different ideas, values, and beliefs, which is a challenge to their own. The deviation from cultural norms gives rise to prejudices and stereotypes of people from a different race, culture, etc. Lipsedge and Littlewood (1989) are among researchers who have discussed the problems faced by those who migrate. The term "culture shock" was used to describe the experience of confusion, rejection, a sense of loss, anxiety, and surprise, among many complex feelings, when encountering a new culture. One has to reinterpret the familiar notion of acceptable behaviour and emotional expression and seek to understand new cues and experiences.

Many protect themselves in the new culture and continue behaving as if they are still living at home. There comes a time, though, that contact with people, places, and practices which are different and often challenging can no longer be avoided. There is great individual and group variation on what value is placed on separating from, or integrating into, the new culture.

The new culture may be rejected completely and perceived as inaccurate, or immigrants may reject their own culture and view the new culture as the ideal place that will offer them good things. Alternatively, there may be a struggle to integrate different elements from both cultures and live in a bicultural environment, or another way of coping may be the complete rejection of both cultures. In the former two patterns, dissociative mechanisms are often utilized, such as idealizing the new culture and regarding what has been left behind as "not-good-enough". Through this process, mourning is avoided, which is intensified if the migration has been a voluntary one. Through the process of splitting, it denies the losses and grief, the anxiety and the guilt which goes with migration. According to Grinberg and Grinberg,

> It becomes essential for the emigrant to maintain the dissociation: good on one side, bad on the other, irrespective of which country represents either characteristics, because if the dissociation breaks down, the inevitable result is confusion and anxiety, with all its feared consequences: one no longer knows who is a friend and who is an enemy, where one can succeed and where one must fail, how to distinguish between the useful and the harmful, how to discriminate between love and hate, life and death. [1989, p. 9]

Pedersen (1996), one of the most prominent researchers and theorists in the cross-cultural field, has challenged the notion that immigrants go through a linear process in adjusting to a new culture. Through extensive research, he reviews the different responses people have to the new culture. He demonstrates how the adjustment process is different for every individual and depends on many different factors. For some people, it may be experienced as very difficult at first, but it may enable them to adjust in the long term. It used to be thought of as people experiencing culture shock during the entry period to a new culture and then, somehow, they overcame this. However, now we know this is a lengthy process, and not necessarily that adjustment improves the longer a person resides in the country. That is, people may feel elated with all the excitement of a new country and a year or two later, or with the break-up of a relationship, suddenly feel "lost", and homesick.

Contrary to the belief that culture shock is a negative experience, sometimes those who have lived through it seem able to adjust more successfully in the long term. There are different models illustrating the adjustment process. For some people, it may be experienced as a "subtractive process", where they may feel that they are subtracting or losing something of their background through the learning of new ideas and experiencing new ways of thinking and behaving. For others, it may be seen as an "additive process", where learning from other cultures is a positive process because the learning from the new culture either complements their own cultural upbringing (and they may even wish to replace some cultural patterns), or they include more traditional patterns that they practise.

Adjustment may also mean having to go through a type of mourning process before one can begin to take on board the new people, places, etc. Kharmi writes of the painful and lonely experience of migration:

> It was a curious thing, when I look back, that not long after we reached Damascus no one spoke of our home any more. Our parents did not talk about Fatima or Muhammad or the house or even Jerusalem. It was as if only I preserved their memory. They seemed wholly preoccupied with the immediate present, as if we had materialized out of nowhere in my grandparents' house . . . and so I took my cue from them and kept my confusion to myself. [2002, p. 138]

Each person, of course, deals with the experience according to her personal psychological resources, that is, the resources she has internalized from the way she was brought up in her family from childhood. Another significant factor is whether there has been support at the time of migration from relations and friends. It is common to have a period of "relapse", as many cross-cultural issues and conflicts are ongoing.

Immigrants, refugees, and exiles can sometimes view the new country as the cause of their problems rather than the country they fled from. However, it is easier for them to see it in this light rather than to have angry feelings for their own country. This process is similar to that experienced by those who have been adopted, who somehow have to make the new parents suffer because, paradoxically, they now feel safer than they felt in the fleeing process. There may be a feeling that they are imprisoned because they have had to leave and that they cannot go back.

Settling into the culture will depend on the links with those left behind and, in turn, the feelings of those left behind towards the emigrant. The reactions about someone leaving may be supportive, critical, anxious, or even envious, and the person may become a scapegoat for taking all the bad away from those who remain so that they can carry on living, or there is projective identification in that there is pleasure in someone who can leave or escape. Those left behind react using defence mechanisms just as much as the person who is leaving. The reactions will be different when there has been a close relationship than when there has been an ambivalent relationship. Those left behind may experience symptoms of hypochondria or real symptoms soon after a loved one's departure. The person leaving may contribute to their reactions by a need to exaggerate what they are leaving behind and what the new place represents. The person may oscillate between a feeling of loss and that of going and relief.

Families

In families or couples there is usually the "executor" of the family's fantasies (Grinberg & Grinberg, 1989). It is particularly difficult if the parents or the partner are the cause of the distress and yet they may be promising a "better future". It may be difficult to grasp the need for the cultural change, and yet they may feel unable to protest. If the instigator or the parents are unable to come to terms with the loss of their country and refuse to become involved in any new "cultural activities", then the others or the children may have to take a similar stance or react against the parents. The family may have full admiration for persons who are seen to "manage" this. Dependants may feel depression, impotence, resentment, and even the wish to take revenge on the executor. There may be disappointment that people did not become more distressed at one's departure.

In some cultures, whole families believe they have to sacrifice their individual needs for the sake of one of the members; for example, the member who seems to be a high achiever in school and is going to change the family's socio-economic status and standing in the community. This inevitably results in a huge amount of pressure if the person does not fulfil their dreams.

To really get into the mind of the immigrant in this scenario, there are interesting texts and films, such as *The Brides* (Scorsese, 2004). This film is set around 1945–1955, when many Greeks wanted to find a better life abroad. The main character, Niki, does not wish to leave her island (Samothrace), but complies with her father's wishes to provide financial support to her poverty-stricken family and marry "over there". When she becomes involved with a foreigner, en route to America, despite her powerful feelings for him, she is determined to fulfil the family's dream and to "maintain the family honour and reputation". The man in question finds it difficult to comprehend this, suggesting that she is now on a ship on the way to America and no longer on Greek soil, so the context has changed and he is expecting her thinking to alter. However, her years of socialization are powerful, and she holds on to her sense of family duty and obligation. She is so deeply saddened by having to leave this man she has fallen in love with that her hair turns grey, and yet she has to sacrifice her personal happiness to fulfil the promise she had made to her family. She portrays a stoic acceptance of her duties. Furthermore, there are clearly the communal elements of the main character, Niki, striking up a friendship with another female from the same culture. Here, the cultural links are shown by the emotions evoked by the character playing "typical island songs" while Niki is attempting to convince her (as much as she is trying to do this to herself) that there is much on offer in the American dream. They may not have communicated in other circumstances back home, but on a foreign land the bond becomes intense and they support each other.

It is quite common to find that families deal with cross-cultural issues through their own systems. They may pass things to other generations, or the parents try to reinforce the characteristics themselves. One of the predominant issues in cross-cultural work is how to tell their children about their culture and to cope with all the fears that they will lose or disrespect their culture. In some cases, the younger generation show more flexibility and ability to learn new customs, even food tastes. Kharmi recalls that after moving to England, she enjoyed the taste of English crumpets. She says,

> I liked them to this day, but my mother, whose taste in food never deviated far from our native Arab cuisine, clearly did not. Later, she adapted the English crumpet into something more fitting to an Arab palate . . . The result was so fundamentally different from the conventional crumpet that it was unrecognizable as such. [2002, p. 178]

Although this seems trivial, it is interesting, as food is such a profound part of our experience. When moving to a new culture, people often try to find food from their culture and it is common that they pack supplies with them. But for some, those who are not acculturated or who are elderly, getting used to something new can be felt to be too much of a task.

In the clinical setting, often the parental loss may be phrased as having concerns about the children, but it can slowly emerge that this is a "smokescreen". For example, a mother who referred her fifteen-year-old son to me for therapy as she felt he was not coping with his schoolwork. I arranged to see her for an initial assessment as she was referring her son, and the more we talked the more it emerged to me how unhappy she was living in London. She had divorced from her husband and did not feel there was anything keeping her here, apart from her son. He was happy to remain here as he was living with his father and visited her during the holidays. The therapy ended up being for her, and she saw me for about eighteen months, after which she decided to move back to Greece.

In children, the loss may be replaced by manic play, or taking the role of the "good child" in order not to worry parents. It is not unusual to have children talking about aliens landing, or spaceships, or being stuck on an aeroplane. There are undoubtedly multiple losses, but we need to find out what kind of loss it is, as it is about people and the places lost. The loss may be about their feeling sad that they cannot convey their cultural experience to peers or their children. An illustration of this is a little girl I worked with many years ago who stopped protesting outwardly (very much modelling her mother's inability to be clear and verbal about her feelings and needs), but experienced steady hair loss. It took some time for the family to come to terms with the cause of this and to discuss openly the family losses. The school can be an enormous support with these issues, and since children spend such a large part of their time at school, it is worth making sure they are aware of any such problems. Nowadays, families can also be helped with books and some appropriate Internet sites, which are aimed at supporting those with similar experiences.

External aspects which contribute to the adjustment process

To feel like oneself, one needs to hold on to the significant elements from the home culture (such as music, objects, myths, landscape). Decorating with objects from home demonstrates a link with the past, links with one's roots, history, and past generations. It becomes extremely important for people to have furniture and belongings around them (Espin, 1992). Those who try to take everything with them try to fill up with the good and familiar things. It is common for people to feel "better" and to report feeling "back to normal" when their belongings have arrived. It is interesting to note what objects those who are migrating (voluntarily, of course), choose to take with them and how they create their new environment. There are those who choose to travel light, and those who pack terribly carefully the significant personal/cultural belongings. For some cultural groups, like Greek Cypriots, roots are very important and ownership of a home and land, which is then passed on to one's children, is very important. As one refugee stated, "I miss my country and my familiar earth" (see personal account of Parvanta, 1992). But, of course, we see that people always re-create something of their culture, but it is exactly a re-creation and not simply transplanting their culture as it was back home. Wishing to hold on to belongings or concrete objects is seen as regressive and not acculturated, and, of course, it can be comforting and healing. The re-creation of the context is critical, and there has to be some room in the therapy to discuss its impact.

In recent times, since communication has improved, people travel, and, of course, the Internet has made a dramatic impact on how people communicate and feel more "in touch". It is astonishing, for example, to find how many people communicate via the Internet. There are numerous web sites for expatriates who communicate with others and share issues. Many share practical information in order to facilitate acculturation in the new environment. This can empower people and provide some kind of context or new meaning for their experiences. Furthermore, satellite television has made it possible for people to keep in touch with media images/news from their own country, on a daily basis if they wish to, as well as accessing cultural materials, such as food or newspapers.

Response of the new culture

Adjustment is also dependent on how the new cultural group behaves, psychologically, physically, and economically. The feelings of being an outsider are also reinforced by the majority culture, which may experience them as "foreign bodies", "aliens" that are threatening, and it becomes safer to keep them at bay. It can alienate different cultural groups further. The immigrant may be viewed as "sensitive" and "needy", and, indeed, this is often the case, as they need more guidance. They will be treated differently if the host community has participated in the arrival of newcomers, for example, by invitation. However, there is often a feeling of intrusion, and it is common that paranoid anxieties of the group increase, with thoughts such as that all the newcomers will take over their jobs. There may be overt or covert hostility, for example, finding it difficult to understand their language, whatever their fluency is like, making gulfs wider by references to historical, political events that they may not be familiar with. Of course, this will also depend on what the newcomers project on to the new environment. Even when there is formal help, it may be difficult for the newcomer to accept it because they feel it is humiliating or that they are being infantilized (that is, as if they are not mature enough emotionally or cognitively), or dehumanized.

One fascinating study by Ritchie and Ritchie (1981) found that Polynesian children were rarely abused. However, when these families were forced to move to areas where there is a predominant western lifestyle, then they found that child abuse became problematic. We may wonder what factors come into play when we read such shocking research on the impact of the environment. It seems that often the societal can support the individual. In one culture, this may be the extended family, which takes care of the children when the mothers are unable to do so due either to psychological or physical absence. In other cases, the communal, literally external, sources take over. The most significant question here is: should care not reflect the needs of the society, or should society reflect the needs of the individual, and is there a balance between these two?

Newly formed families do not start as blank screens. They have been influenced both consciously and unconsciously by the external environment, usually their closest care-givers. To some degree, they will all re-enact family scripts, whether these were construc-tive or unsuitable. We certainly know that those who are supported by the external environment, perhaps partners or friends, can be prevented from re-enacting powerful generational dynamics, such as neglect or abuse.

Racism

Although there is a more comprehensive discussion of racism in other chapters of this text (see Chapters Two and Eleven), it is such a significant factor in our clients' lives that is important to revisit it briefly in this section. This is in order to remind us that many ethnic minority groups experience social deprivation in many spheres of their lives, including housing, education, employment, and health care. Many therapists state that they are not racist because it is asso-ciated with being an external or socio-political issue. However, when one begins to take the issues on board, the political filters into the psychological. Racism is everyone's concern because it is linked with human deprivation, a hierarchical system, and lack of human freedom and dignity. Racism creates feelings of envy, anger, jeal-ousy, aggression, greed, deprivation, mistrust, fear, and powerless-ness, and it is vital that is worked with on interpsychic and intra-psychic levels. A most poignant account of the impact of racism (and, although dated, it reminds us of the impact of racism which takes place today, perhaps in more subtle forms) comes from the psychoanalyst Fanon (1991), in his internationally acclaimed book *Black Skin, White Masks*, an analysis of the effect of colonial oppres-sion on the human psyche. It is a personal account of his experi-ences: despite his French education, he was rejected in France by the French because of skin colour.

Issues of residing in the culture: permanent or temporary stay?

A theme that is very poignant for many ethnic minorities is the hoped for return "back home". It is common to hear people say that one day they will return home, and many years later may still be away and many never do return. This is an issue for both the second or third generation immigrants and for their parents. The children have built up ties in the new environment that include their parents. However, if the parents decide to return to the homeland, many of the children go through tremendous feelings of loss, and even guilt that they are not "good-enough" somehow to make the parents remain in the new homeland. For the parents, the return is equally difficult, as the homeland is now different and brings a new emotional upheaval. If they have had influences from mainly one culture during their earlier years, they often adapt better than the younger ones, who have got used to other cultures (Eakin, 1996). But for those who have really taken on a new identity, there will be struggles.

> Neither those who left nor those who stayed at home are the same: everyone has felt the impact of the separation, and beneath the surface, each reproaches the other for having abandoned him. Nearly everything must be rebuilt, like a house after a tempest: fallen trees cleared away, cracked roofs repaired, rubble swept away. And as for the structure itself surely a different house is needed, for the returning person inhabits a different reality. The one thing certain is they will feel a new kind of homesickness, a new kind of grief. [Grinberg & Grinberg, 1989, p. 188]

Through theory and clinical vignettes, this chapter has illustrated that people react differently to cultural moves. The different patterns are paths that individuals choose, but one individual may alternate views at different times taking a different amount of time to adjust. In fact, most people change views according to the environment they are in. This is a way of dealing with conflicting values, ideas, and traditions that had never been questioned before. Hence, the process of acculturation can occur on different levels for different areas (for example one can be acculturated in terms of friendships, but not in terms of ethnic choice of partner), and it is by no means directional with a common outcome. Whatever form it takes, people need time when they are going through the adjustment process, sometimes a rather prolonged period of adjustment.

Psycho-social issues shared by different groups of ethnic minorities

This section will be an overview of the psycho-social issues faced by different types of immigrants: first generation immigrants, second generation immigrants, those who had a (level of) choice in leaving their culture will have different psychological needs to those who left due to abrupt, involuntary conditions like a natural disaster or a war situation (the latter will be discussed in more detail in Chapters Nine and Ten). Additionally, there will be an overview of the psycho-social issues shared by mixed race individuals, international students, and guest workers. Although this chapter takes us through the general issues shared by these ethnic groups, the clinical cases concentrate on the unique combination and meanings of these dynamics for an individual and how they manifest in the transtherapeutic encounter.

First generation immigrants

Clients who are first generation may be perceived as belonging to one national category and they may, in fact, adhere to another. For example, they may define themselves as "black British" or "Afro-British", while they may be labelled by society as "black", or they may define themselves as "Muslim" or "Hindu", while they are labelled by others under the vast and rather anonymous umbrella "Asian", which, in fact, consists of more than one hundred sub-groups, languages, and traditions.

Many immigrants speak of the importance of bringing up children according to their own culture in a way that surprises them. One South American woman in her mid-twenties said to me that she did not realize how important her roots were to her until she had children. Having children means different things for different people, but there is often a view that it is a way of continuing the family and the culture. In Britain, it is common that Cypriot children attend an English school during the week and Greek school on Saturdays, which is where the active cultural transmission is taking place. Children learn to speak Greek, they learn about the culture and customs, including Greek dances and cooking. For those who chose to emigrate because of financial factors, there is the wish for the children somehow not to have to suffer as the parents did. This can put a great deal of pressure on them to do well at school, and not only to do well, but to excel in their future jobs.

This may be particularly significant for those women who have been separated from their husbands for the first time, or who have to go out to work. It may mean that they are the breadwinners for the first time. The home sphere is the only area of control for some women who have never worked outside the home. The men were the mediators between the outside world and the home. All of a sudden, they find themselves having to communicate and interact with others in a completely different sphere.

An individual who is brought up within two cultural systems may exercise a choice in what they practise and what values they will follow or pass on to their children. However, it is common that individuals who are seen (in everyday encounters or by therapists) as acculturated are not given the opportunity to talk about their own cultural heritage and experiences. Casas and Pytluk point out that

> Identification within any culture is essentially independent of iden-
> tification with any culture. In other words identifying with one
> culture in no way diminishes the ability of an individual to identify
> with any other culture. [1995, p. 173]

Second and third generation immigrants

Second or third generation immigrants have their own unique issues: it is not clear when they stop being called "minorities" or being seen as different. In many contexts, they are no longer migrants, as it is assumed they are growing up in one environment and not moving into other cultures. But I would argue that they are also "immigrants" in some way, because they have to negotiate different types of cultures on a different scale, every day. The home can represent one reality and the majority culture another reality, which hold distinct values. There may be conflict in terms of religious ideology between the two, different behaviours are permitted/discouraged and exhibited or remain hidden, different ways of thinking and language are used, among many other differences. Often second generation immigrants can become the mediators between the new culture and their mother culture, literally by being the ones who communicate and arrange matters outside the home and even psychologically almost buffer the other members of the family, usually older members, from the new practices.

The younger members of the ethnic minority communities, in particular, can start behaving like chameleons. This is in order to cope with the contradictions found when they try to incorporate more than one set of cultural beliefs. They may be more flexible and find creative ways to adjust more easily than the older immigrants, but there is a danger that this may be at a cost. Thomas (1995) talks about the "proxy self" that may develop, where the chameleon state is taken to such an extreme that the child strongly wants to believe they belong to another culture or race and resents their own. Although people (irrespective of their age) may wish to be associated with only one cultural or racial group and become rather resentful about being seen as "foreign", this may change later. Parents may also feel they are the only ones who are trying hard to maintain the cultural values. It may result in attempts to encourage the children to mix more with the same cultural group peers, and not only regulating, but in some cases prohibiting, meetings with majority culture peers outside school hours. For example, Greek children who are sent to Greek school on Saturdays may view it as time away from their main school friends and play since it is an extra-curricular activity. As a consequence, they may resist attending or become unruly and disruptive at the school (Constantinides, 1991). Although, children may find it easier if they have been brought up with acculturated parents who convey one model of functioning and the gap between school and home life is less marked these are difficult and often painful parenting decisions. This issue remains controversial as to how much children need to know and understand about their cultural and racial roots.

Case vignettes

Gita

Gita came to see me for problems in her relationship. She was second generation Indian and was involved with an Indian man. In the beginning of the therapy, she appeared rather "westernized" in her thinking, cultural mannerisms, and dress code. During the initial sessions, she spoke in a highly academic manner and did not refer to her feelings or make any reference to her ethnic background, despite my attempt to find out more about her upbringing influences. After about a month into the therapy, her father fell ill and shortly after was diagnosed as suffering from leukaemia. Gita was devastated by the news and feared the worst. He was hospitalized soon after his diagnosis and Gita spent most evenings by his bedside at the hospital. Those few weeks after her father's diagnosis seemed to have triggered off a great deal of cultural material in our sessions that she had not referred to before. For example, she had never visited India, as her parents had always wished for her to become "fully integrated in British society". Even her partner had urged for them to make a joint visit, but she had always underestimated its importance. After her father died, she carried on coming to see me for a few months where she mourned her father. What she had not anticipated was that she was also mourning for the cultural heritage she had not really allowed herself to experience, as it was easier to cope with one set of values. Her partner had been the link with the new culture and her father was the link with the Indian culture, religion, and language. She saw her mother as the emotional support and her father as helping her to become socially and politically aware. She felt quite "special" as the only one who engaged in these socio-political discussions, unlike her siblings. However, this was almost something private between the two of them, and when he became ill she felt very alone.

She wrote to me once we ended therapy to tell me how she had decided it was time to visit India, to see her parents' birthplace and meet some of her relations. She planned to stay there for a few months. On her return, she was in touch with me (as we had planned) and came back to see me for a few final sessions. The change in her was striking. She had grown her hair in the time that we had not met and wore a sari. I was struck at how relaxed she seemed in it. She talked of how India had opened up a whole new way of life for her and she was able to make links with her parental culture. When I commented on how different she seemed and that the visit to India seemed to have had a profound effect on her, she cried. Her tears were an enormous relief, being a reflection of the potential loss had she not reconnected with the richness of her parental culture. She realized how much had not been considered in the past, and yet her childhood cultural influences had had a significant impact on her identity. There was recognition that there was still a long path ahead. She felt she could proceed to take on board her different cultural worlds with the (new-found) support of peers of the same "mixture" of cultures as herself. Through the therapeutic process, she felt she gained the resources to deal with her conflicts. Moreover, she had the insight that the new cultural richness may bring other conflicts in the future, but for now every-thing felt more manageable.

However, even if there has not been any explicit discussion of the second and third generations' roots, it is common that much has been transmitted. It is common around adolescence or during a life loss; people seek to know more about their cultural and racial ancestry. There are intergenerational influences, linked with power-ful or traumatic historical events that sometimes influence the second and third generations at an even deeper level. A good exam-ple of how racial and cultural material is transmitted through the generations is the children and grandchildren of parents who were Jewish holocaust survivors. The powerful feeling of survivor guilt is something that still remains a rather secretive issue, and yet it can preoccupy the younger generations even though they have not witnessed the horrors of their parents or grandparents. One of my clients, John, told me right from the beginning of the therapeutic relationship that the events of the Holocaust were something that he grew up with. He could not remember when he had first heard about it, as it is something that he has always had with him. He said that his father reminded them of the Holocaust, and it felt almost as if they had a memorial in the house and you could never get too carried away with laughter as you would be reminded of what the living family generations symbolized.

Another example of traumatic historical events being transmit-ted occurs with black clients who, at some point of considerable work in psychotherapy (this has certainly been reported by many therapists; see Chapter Thirteen in this text) might make a reference to slavery and the racial ancestry of black people. As Pajaczkowska and Young say:

> Slavery racially destabilized Africa and resulted in the undermin-ing and fragmentation of cultural self identity both for those who underwent the process of dispersal and disruption and for their descendants. Black people are frequently in the position of having to piece together distorted fragments of the past and of past selves in order to re-create a self-determined picture of individual and collective cultural identities. Reclamation of the past through "remembering" is considered to be virtually a moral obligation by some African-Americans since the official histories have failed to document and acknowledge the meanings of the experiences of their ancestors. [1992, p. 210]

International students and guest workers

There are pressures on international students (see Khoo, Abu-Rasain, & Hornby, 2002) to achieve as financial and social investments have been made by parents in order to send them abroad. There is often the experience of culture shock, which raises the question of what do they do to retain identity. There are separations and exploring an environment away from family for the first time. Students often come to the countries that originally colonized their countries of origin, with the view of gaining a good education. This may evoke feelings of inferior/superior culture. They may experience being different, or experience racism for the first time, or engage in a cross-cultural/racial relationship for the first time. This is often a common area for those young people who come to therapy. There are many anxieties about returning home. My experience is that towards the end of the studies, issues of identity are magnified for international students, as they now have to face the return to their home country and reunion with family and the old cultural context (Eleftheriadou, 1996).

For those who choose to move because of economic factors or educational factors, the experience may be quite different, in that they often see the new culture as their host culture for a few years, with specific goals to fulfil. They wish to gain the culture's good aspects and not have any involvement in other areas. Similarly, for those who seek work abroad, it may be seen as a temporary sacrifice to gain experience or improve their financial situation and return to the home country. The impact may be greater for their partners, the many women who accompany them abroad and lose their own jobs and status, and it may take a long time before they are able to find employment, if this is possible in the new country. Those who travel because of their jobs face quite different issues, because, although much may be lost, there may be gain in their new career opportunities.

People with a biracial or bicultural/mixed identity

Demographic trends indicate that mixed race children are increasing rapidly as more people intermarry we have more mixed racial/ cultural relationships. This increase suggests that it is now time that the issues are examined more closely. People of mixed parentage ιve to integrate two or more racial and cultural backgrounds from ϳirth. This means that their gender and ethnic identification process is rather more complicated than children who are brought up in monoracial or cultural families. Mixed race children often experience the same degree of discrimination as ethnic minority groups. They tend to experience different levels of discrimination depending on their racial composition. Nevertheless, often, whatever colour of skin they have, they are perceived to be black. There is the myth that they must identify with only one group (Kerwin & Ponterotto, 1995), which, of course, would deny the heritage of one parent. There is very little research and literature on individuals who have mixed racial or cultural parentage and the implications of their identity formation. The available research has tended to view them as "marginal", as they are neither "black" nor "white", and to believe that mixed parentage has negative implications on their identity. However, work by Tizard and Phoenix (1989) has introduced a different picture. In one study, they saw fifty-eight young people aged 15–16 years. They all had one parent who was white and one who was either black African or Afro-Caribbean. Just under half of the group perceived themselves as "black". The rest saw themselves as "coloured", "brown", or "half and half". Interestingly, none of them described themselves as "white", although they were aware of having a white part. About two-thirds of them were very positive about their mixed race, but they seemed to have had a more negative perception when younger. Interestingly, half of them had wanted to be white when they were much younger. They seemed to have experienced more problems than either white or black groups. Different factors, such as the parental attitudes to their mixed race, relationships with their parents, social class background, schooling environment, and, inevitably, societal perceptions and racism, contributed to their identity development. The study of the psychology and social position of mixed race individuals has had much impact in understanding their needs and, on a social policy level, has helped to inform adoption, fostering, and psychotherapy practice.

Clinical case material

Mixed race identity formation in the context of different racial/ cultural contexts is demonstrated in the case of Michael, a mixed-race adolescent, Rosa, who struggled between her parental English and Spanish cultures, and Jackie, who was brought up with only one white parent and felt rather confused about her black heritage due to its absence.

Michael

One of my young clients, Michael, who is an adolescent of mixed race, was sent to therapy after many changes of his foster home placements. After about the fourth session, we began to talk about his upbringing and how many different families he had had to get used to. I asked about the racial background of the families and he said they had all been black, but his current foster mother was white. He went on to say that there was no one who was mixed race like himself, and I asked him what that felt like. At first he said it did not matter, but later told me that they always saw him as black. I then wondered how he saw himself. He said "I am mixed race of course!" He then asked me whether I was mixed race. Before I even had a chance to gather my thoughts, he said, "But of course you are mixed race *and* Greek." We discussed what this meant and it is interesting how in one way he viewed us as having similar experiences and in another I was also different. Michael had a West Indian father and a white mother and he never really saw how the two of them were together. As a result, he would often enquire whether I got on with my black colleagues, and one day he broached the subject of race with a curiosity about the "black man I saw in the waiting room at Nafsiyat". Once again his comment gave us the opportunity to explore his internal racial identity, what he had experienced externally, as well as our relationship. Of course our relationship was complicated as we were two people from different races/cultures who were together and communicating in a way that his parents never had towards each other or towards him (they had never respected each other's racial background or his mixed ancestry). All of these racial issues intensified his psychological history—a child who had not known any stable parental figures—and as a result he held an extremely negative image of himself both emotionally and racially.

Rosa

One woman, in her late thirties, came to me to discuss her relationships. She repeatedly believed that none of the men she dated would ever really understand her cultural background. In the beginning of relationships, she would describe things as going well, but that they would get to a point where there would be an "unbridgeable difference". We had to work on the pain that she felt and her great isolation in relation to these cultural issues. These were placed on others and she did not give them a chance to understand. In fact, she confirmed this to herself by being alone, which was the very thing she was frightened of being.

In our work, we had to uncover what these cultural issues meant and whether they were really unbridgeable. In one sense, she had to understand why, even with men of her own culture, she felt "different". She was certainly caught between two cultures, but it was difficult to accept that she could take from both and also reject elements from both. As with all cultural issues, there were also family issues that contributed to this feeling of being "in-between". Her parents, a Spanish mother and British father, had divorced in her late teens, and she had always lived "in-between" the two parents.

She found it hard that they would always present themselves as a united front, almost as if they were one person. This outward presentation did not match with all the difficulties they had, their arguments and her father's physical attacks when he was drunk. Patients can end up taking on something of the parents and not realize it in any conscious way. As a result, it ended up inhabiting her life. She was slowly more able to manage it in therapy.

In the case of Rosa, she had been relieved when her parents divorced, because in some way they were two people again. When they finally developed separate houses and lives, she was relieved, but then it pushed her into a depression. It was as if she was lost and did not know which path to follow, as if she had different personalities who belonged to different cultures. For example, her mother made links again with Spain, and was debating whether to re-root herself there. This external event also threw Rosa, as she needed to find her own roots.

This has many themes in common with clients who find themselves growing up biculturally, but the parents have not been able to hold on to the mixedness. The mixedness can be taken into consideration if the parents are able to hold in mind each other's culture in a positive way. If the parents are not able to do this, and, in fact, the child picks up hostile feelings about the other parent, they will internalize that part of themselves in a similar way.

This is similar for other issues of mixed race, but it is much more pronounced with those who are overtly mixed. Societal influences will also have a great impact in facilitating a positive or more negative view.

Jackie

Jackie, a woman in her early twenties, came to see me after a decision to move from home. She had grown up with her mother and her mother's white boyfriend until she was about six years old, and then she moved in with her aunt. It was thought that her aunt could take better care of her since she was older than her mother. Her aunt was also used to children, since she had two children of her own. Jackie had regular, but rather infrequent, contact with her mother, which had begun to upset her a great deal. Many of the feelings about her own mother had been triggered by her own pregnancy and subsequent miscarriage. She had had ambivalent feelings about her own pregnancy; a part of her desperately wanted a child, and another part felt that she was not ready. She was not in a position to support a child financially or psychologically. She felt far too insecure in her relationship to expect support from her partner. Initially, her partner made it clear that he did not want her to go ahead with the pregnancy, but in the end had left it up to her to decide. She had almost decided to have a termination of the pregnancy when she had a miscarriage. She felt guilty after the miscarriage, although she was also aware that if she had had the baby she would have repeated her mother's footsteps, as she also had become pregnant in a loveless relationship where her partner did not wish to take part in the parenting or support her in any way.

In one session, she talked with great distress of an event she had attended with her mother. She was devastated by the fact that many people did not know who she was, and when she explained people would be surprised, and she felt she had to go through explanations of the living arrangements. She desperately wanted to be part of a family and to be included in her mother's family. She always said how dearly she loved her aunt and she was very grateful to her for everything she had done, but she wished her relationship with her own parents was closer. Everyone from her mother's family, especially her aunt, saw her as white and gave her "white food" and spoke "white language". She was viewed as "black" by other white people, however, and when they would go out people would show the inevitable surprise about her being a different colour to her mother. She could not feel she was either one or the other, however. Recently, she would frequently get rather upset that she was not "black enough", and that somehow she would be "found out". When we explored this further, she was anxious that people might ask her questions about socio-political events and practices in the West Indies that she might not be able to answer accurately or with much detail.

Towards the end of her therapy, Jackie felt that she had a clearer identity, although she acknowledged that since she was a combination of two racial heritages, however much she could integrate the two, she would always be a "mixture" to others. All the issues relating to her racial identity were linked to a time where she was thinking of leaving home, and this brought into question where she belonged and how she wanted to live. Many other issues emerged about being brought up by a very young mother, a teenager, who could not really fulfil all her needs and facilitate her psychological and social–racial identity development. In fact she had always picked up mum's strong negative feelings about her father, and found it difficult to separate the "father" part she had inherited from her father from her mother's perception. She was also at a similar age to when her parents had met and became involved. When she was younger, she had wanted to be white, but as she grew older she felt less and less need to be different. Everything she knew about her identity she had found out on her own by having black and mixed race female friends. She was able to explore a different social sphere to that of her aunt's family because she could use her aunt as a safe psychological base to return to.

During the sessions, she made contact with her father and told him much of what she had felt. They had not met for a few years, after a big argument where Jackie had been furious with him. To her surprise, he became distressed by her telephone call and asked to meet with her soon after. When they met, Jackie felt something had lifted from her. She did not get the explanations she would have wanted, but she was able to understand more about him and his relationship with her mother. She felt she had much to learn about her cultural heritage from her father's side and enquired about other family members whom she had never met. She knew that she would never relive all the years she had missed with her father, but at least they could try to maintain more contact and get to know each other more now.

She found it useful to work with me because she did not see me as one or the other, black or white, although she did perceive me as being different from her. I experienced this as having an appropriate distance where she could reflect, and, at the same time, she could feel intimate with me and that I would have an understanding of what it was to be "mixed". Towards the end of the therapy, she felt she was more integrated in terms of all the different components; the white part and her mother and the black part and her father. Jackie had experienced many losses in her life; she had grown up with little experience of mothering and even less of fathering, and had very little information about her black heritage. Through therapy she was able to experience a certain level of mothering from me and, at the same time, a vital exploration into her fragmented racial and cultural identity.

Global nomads

There is an increasing group of people, internationally, who would classify themselves as "global nomads". For these people, who have grown up as multi-cultural children, migration becomes part of their lifestyle and, hence, it has been listed here as a separate category. One has to just look at the number of websites under the headings of migration issues, expatriates, international students, and global childhoods, among many, to see how this multi-cultural group has grown. Seaman, writing about his own travelling childhood, says,

> We learned early that "home" was an ambiguous concept, and wherever we lived, some essential part of our lives was always somewhere else, happy and sad at the same time. . . . We learned to be independent and we learned that things were out of our control. We learned the reassuring familiarity of routine and the comforting exactness of being able to pack everything needed for life into a single footlocker and bedroll. [1996, p. 46]

Another example is a colleague of mine who had moved around a great deal, who said to me, "I suppose there is just something inside me that makes me move around a lot and it is so part of me I can't change it" (or maybe a wish not to change it and to examine this need, as it serves a particular purpose at that time). This statement was made by a man who, from his early years, had been brought up moving from country to country, because his father had been in the army. For him, moving was not just an option, but deeply rooted in his need for new experiences and relationships. This, of course, can have the flip side also, where there are constantly broken relationships. Some have called such people "global nomads", as they move so often. Pollock (1994) captures the experiences of the global nomads, referring to the concept of "multiple grief". This implies that although they have learned some multi-cultural skills and appear to settle quickly in new environments, there is still repeated loss: often a simultaneous saying good-bye to friends, family, the climate, having to let go of what they have got used to as to how people interact, food that has become familiar, and there is even loss of the surrounding landscape, among many other things (in my clinical work, it is small details that are missed, as they matter to people). Something unfamiliar puts the brain into more of a state of "being on guard" than relaxed. These goodbyes are intense, because the relationships with people are close, their feelings can remain unresolved, as they may not have been permitted to mourn, and, finally, this is a lonely process, as they may not share with anyone other than their parents or partners if they have joined them.

Even after many years, one can feel that "home" is their country of origin, and even though outwardly they can appear to be integrated (and, indeed, they may take part in, and actively contribute to, many aspects of the new culture), deep down they do not feel that they have the same ownership rights. Mukherjee, writing about the USA, states, "it was their country and we were the interlopers, and in their hearts and in their history it is still their land" (1999, p. 86).

Conclusion

In conclusion, this chapter provides an overview of some of the common group psycho-social experiences. The ability to maintain old attachments or form new attachments with people of the same/ different cultural backgrounds depends on individual factors, such as one's personality, previous and current support systems, the capacity to be resourceful and use resources, and also the type of psychosocial resources available to them and how accessible these are made (see counselling service model of Mothertongue, Chapter Eight).

Entering a new culture is undoubtedly an exhausting time, even if exciting and a conscious choice. There is a parallel of this new experience with babies and their need to sleep so much in the first three days after birth, as if to rest from the difficult and unknown journey. They need much more holding during this time, and then they can proceed with exploring the new environment. Migrants who have the luxury of this space, like the baby who can sleep, may find they are able to gain strength to explore properly. Those preoccupied with finances, or finding work, may not have this space, and become quite overwhelmed with the newness of everything around them. Therefore, the adjustment period is quite a delicate stage, and might determine how they settle, influencing the decision to remain or return back home. If it is facilitated for the individual/group, it is a smoother process, but if the family is threatened by the perceived changes, then it creates lasting turmoil for the individual.

References

Akhtar, S. (1999). *Immigration and Identity, Turmoil, Treatment and Transformation*. Oxford: Jason Aronson.

Berry, J. W., Poortinga, Y. H., Segall, M. H., & Dasen, P. R. (1992). *Cross-cultural Psychology*. New York: Cambridge University Press.

Bion, W. (1970). *Attention and Interpretation*. London: Tavistock.

Casas, J. M., & Pytluk, S. D. (1995). Hispanic identity development: implications for research and practice. In: J. G. Ponterotto, J. M. Casa, L. A. Suzuki, & C. M. Alexander (Eds.), *Handbook of Multicultural Counselling* (pp. 155–180). London: Sage.

Constantinides, P. (1991). The Greek Cypriots: factors in the maintenance of ethnic identity. In: J. L. Watson (Ed.), *Between Two Cultures: Migrants and Minorities in Britain* (pp. 269–300). London: Blackwell [reprinted London: W. W. Norton , 1998].

Eakin, K. B. (1996). You can't go home again. In: C. Smith (Ed.), *Strangers at Home* (pp. 57–80). Bayside, New York: Aletheia.

Eleftheriadou, Z. (1995). Psycho-social aspects of thalassaemia: a psychodynamic understanding. *Psychodynamic Counselling*, 2: 283–286.

Eleftheriadou, Z. (1996). Notions of culture. In: S. Sharples (Ed.), *Changing Cultures: Developments in Cross-Cultural Theory and Practice* (pp. 7–13). London: UKCOSA.

Espin, O. M. (1992). The roots uprooted: the psychological impact of historical/political dislocation. In: E. Cole, O. M. Espin, & E. D. Rothblum (Eds.), *Refugee Women and Their Mental Health: Shattered Societies, Shattered Lives* (pp. 9–20). London: Harrington Park Press.

Fanon, F. (1991). *Black Skins, White Masks*. London: Pluto Press.

Grinberg, L., & Grinberg, R. (1989). *Psychoanalytic Perspectives on Migration and Exile*. London: Yale University Press.

Kerwin, C., & Ponterotto, J. G. (1995). Biracial identity development. In: J. G. Ponterotto, J. M. Casa, L. A. Suzuki, & C. M. Alexander (Eds.), *Handbook of Multicultural Counselling* (pp. 199–217). London: Sage.

Kharmi, G. (2002). *In Search of Fatima: A Palestinian Story*. London: Verso.

Khoo, P. L. S., Abu-Rasain, M. H., & Hornby, G. (2002). Counselling foreign students: a review of strategies. In: S. Palmer (Ed.), *Multicultural Counselling: A Reader* (pp. 98–130). London: Sage.

Littlewood, R., & Lipsedge, M. (1989). *Aliens and Alienists*. London: Unwin Hyman.

Mukherjee, B. (1999). Imagining homelands. In: A. Aciman (Ed.), *Letters of Transit: Reflections on Exile, Identity, Language and Loss* (pp. 65–86). New York: New Press.

Pajaczkowska, C., & Young, L. (1992). Racism, representation, psychoanalysis. In: J. Donald & A. Rattansi (Eds.), *Race, Culture and Difference* (pp. 198–219). London, Sage.

Parvanta, S. (1992). The balancing act: plight of Afghan women refugees. In: E. Cole, O. M. Espin, & E. D. Rothblum (Eds.), *Refugee Women and Their Mental Health: Shattered Societies, Shattered Lives* (pp. 113–128). London: Harrington Park Press.

Pedersen, P. (1996). Recent trends and developments in cross-cultural theories. In: S. Sharples (Ed.), *Changing Cultures: Developments in Cross-cultural Theory and Practice* (pp. 14–31). London: UKCOSA.

Pollock, J. (1994). In: K. C. McCluskey (Ed.), *Notes from a Travelling Childhood* (pp. 72–74). Washington, DC: A Foreign Service Youth Foundation Publication.

Ritchie, J., & Ritchie, J. (1981). Child rearing and child abuse. The Polynesia context. In: J. E. Korbin (Ed.), *Child Abuse and Neglect across Cultural Perspectives* (pp. 186–204). Berkeley. CA: University of California Press.

Scorsese, M. (2004). *The Brides* (film). Directed by Pantelis Voulgaris & Martin Scorsese. US/Greece: Alco Films.

Seaman, P. A. (1996). Rediscovering a sense of place. In: C. Smith (Ed,), *Strangers at* Home (pp. 36–56). New York: Aletheia.

Thomas, L. (1995). Psychotherapy in the context of race and culture: an inter-cultural therapeutic approach. In: S. Fernando (Ed.), *Mental Health in a Multi-Ethnic Society* (pp. 172–190). London: Routledge.

Tizard, B., & Phoenix, A. (1989). Black identity and transracial adoption. *New Community, 15*: 427–437.

Verne, J. (2005). *Around the World in Eighty Days*. London: CRW Publishing.

Winnicott, D. (1958). *Collected Papers: Through Paediatrics to Psycho-Analysis*. London: Tavistock.

Winnicott, D. (1971). *Playing and Reality*. London: Routledge.

CHAPTER EIGHT

A working model of a community based, culturally sensitive counselling service

Beverley Costa

Introduction

This chapter outlines the development and the delivery of a culturally sensitive counselling service, in response to the needs of Black and Minority Ethnic (BME) communities, entitled Mothertongue. Clinical examples and experiences are used to illustrate the way in which a bridge is forged between clinical and community development work, in order to provide a relevant service to the target client group. It examines how the therapeutic boundaries have to be renegotiated, as the work is located in a particular social and political context.

Origins and need for the service

Over a number of years, there had been growing concern on the part of professionals in health and social care that the ethnic minority communities in Reading were not receiving the type of help with mental health issues that they needed. Ethnic minorities in Reading account for some 13% of the population, and they were barely figuring on the statistics for clients attending local counselling services.

Some assumptions of traditional counselling services are that:

- clients will seek counselling when they need it;
- clients will make their way to the clinic for the counselling sessions;
- clients will trust that the service will be confidential;
- psychological or emotional issues only will be attended to in the counselling session; practical problems will be dealt with elsewhere.

Traditionally, unless associated with a specific social issue, for example, domestic violence or substance abuse, they have seldom been organizations that focus on community engagement.

From consultation with the community, we learned that language, cultural beliefs (about distress and help seeking), stigma, concerns about confidentiality, and a fear of an imposition of Western views (British Psychodrama Association, Cross Cultural and Equality Consultative Committee, 2003) were barriers to obtaining service provision from mainstream service providers. Social and economic deprivation was also identified as an additional barrier to accessing services.

Learning from this feedback, the organization decided to take a community development approach to the creation of a community service, the fundamental aspect of which is the Mothertongue Counselling and Listening Service. The Mothertongue Counselling Service has developed a model of counselling which is appropriate for the clients from BME communities with whom they work.

The counselling service model

The model developed by the Mothertongue Counselling Service enables us to provide a professional culturally sensitive service where people can be heard with respect in the language of their choice. We do this by attending to the pre-therapeutic session material, the material of the therapeutic session, and the wider social frame.

Pre-therapeutic session material

Client engagement

The person-centred model, Rogers (1951), highlights the need to meet the person where they are. If we are only to wait for them in the consulting room, we may never get to meet them at all. Our experiences showed us that people from BME communities were not accessing help from early intervention services, such as counselling organizations for emotional and mental distress. They were presenting at mental health services in crisis, once the police or emergency department of the hospital had been involved.

We believed that it would be essential to find ways of reaching out to these communities in order to engage them in the counselling service provision. This, in part, led to our decision to locate the counselling service within a "community service framework" (described in greater detail later in this chapter).

As part of the counselling process, we have also found it useful to include for some people an educational component about the nature of counselling and the professional boundaries within which we operate. This is because different cultures may have different expectations around time and the concept of appointments. While we recognize, respect, and work with the fact that people have many constraints on them, for example, asylum seekers have to attend appointments with lawyers and the Home Office over which they have little control, we are clear about communicating our terms of working. This means that clients know what to expect from us. We also let our clients know that in order to use our resources effectively, we have an appointment system, and that it is important for people to make every effort to keep appointments or to keep us informed if they need to cancel. Almost invariably, clients understand, accept, and respect this.

We have found that many of our clients need much reassurance about confidentiality. However, there may be mistrust within the community that is so deep-seated that potential clients will not use the service. It can be particularly reassuring for people in very small, close-knit communities to find that the available counsellors do not live in the immediate vicinity and are located outside the client's community's social or familial networks.

Some of our clients find it difficult to trust professionals and to believe that we will work to our guidelines on confidentiality. Those who fled violence and war in their home countries may have been betrayed by people in whom they had placed their trust. Many BME communities are often very small. People are used to sharing much of their lives together when they want to, and even when they do not. The concept of professional counselling confidentiality may also be new for some people, who may have had experiences where it was not always possible to trust that professionals would remain impartial. In these circumstances, it is important to allow the opportunity for people to engage slowly and tentatively with the counselling sessions, and then they can slowly reassure themselves that this is a safe relationship. The following example, of Hasan, may help to illustrate this.

Hasan

Hasan, a nineteen-year-old male asylum seeker, agreed to access counselling at the suggestion of his support worker. She accompanied him for the first time at his request. He was unsure at this first session whether he felt counselling would be of any benefit for him. It was certainly not a form of helping with which he was familiar from his home country, and he was not sure what he would get from the counselling sessions that he was not already getting from the support worker, whom he already trusted and respected. Nevertheless, he agreed to give it a try, as there was nothing else on offer and he was experiencing very high levels of anxiety. After one or two more sessions, he felt able to attend on his own, although he found it difficult to stay for more than twenty minutes at a session. He seemed to be finding some comfort from knowing that the counsellor was still there each week. This, in itself, was perhaps the therapeutic function of the session. Perhaps he needed to test out the reliability of the counsellor. For this young man, who had lost so many of his family, it may have been reassuring to know, if difficult to trust, that the counsellor was still around each week even if he was unable to engage in anything deeper at this stage. Over a period of weeks, this changed for him, and he began to engage more fully in the therapeutic process, attending for the full amount of time for each session. This seemed to form part of the engagement process with this highly traumatized young man. He was able to enter tentatively into the therapy on terms that he could relate to. Over a period of months, the counsellor was able to support him through a series of failed appeals he was submitting regarding his claim for asylum. He eventually won his case, and he quoted the fact that the counsellor had been alongside him throughout his journey. This was the one thing that had stopped him from, in his words, "going out of my mind".

The material of the therapeutic session

Use of the mother tongue ("one's native language", The New Shorter Oxford English Dictionary, 1993, p. 1837) and working with interpreters

In order to meet people where they are, we also need to be able to speak a common language. Where people are able to speak in their mother tongue, they may find that they are able to access their emotions more readily (Shaikh, 1999). Therefore, we use bi/trilingual counsellors, so that we are able to work directly in ten languages.

We have also developed a model for counsellors and interpreters who work together. This is an area that has been written about by others, including Fox (2001), and Tribe and Raval (2003). Our model is a collaborative one, where the interpreter and counsellor work together as a team. Integral to any counselling session where an interpreter is used is pre-planning time (even more essential if it is the first time a counsellor and interpreter have worked together). At this meeting, the two professionals need to agree on the way that they are going to work together; for example, how the session will begin and close, a clarification of their roles and responsibilities, and the nature of their relationship with the client.

We ask for everything spoken in the room to be translated, so that everyone is kept fully informed in the session. Also, we ask that the interpreter not be working with that particular client in any other capacity. We have found that if an interpreter has any kind of relationship with the client outside of the counselling session, it can seriously undermine the therapeutic work. For many clients, the counselling session is the only safe space they have away from all the other aspects of their lives. Although it is accepted that the emotions may flow more readily when speaking in one's mother tongue, it will often not be possible to match the client's language needs and the service's ability to provide the appropriate language. The most important aspect is the ability for the client and counsellor to be able to form a "therapeutic alliance" (see Chapter Six). Although clients may prefer to be able to speak in their own mother tongue, once they have formed a relationship with a counsellor they prefer to remain with their original counsellor. Clients who have conducted their counselling in (sometimes quite limited) English report back the following: "I feel my counsellor really believed my story when no one else was listening", or "I felt understood from the heart".

Sometimes, counselling has begun with the use of an interpreter and then, for practical reasons, it has needed to continue without them. In a number of cases, we have found that this has had a useful outcome. The initial trust-building and background story gathering has been helped by the communication support provided by an interpreter. Once the interpreter was no longer present, clients often felt freer to talk about much more emotionally charged material directly with the counsellor.

Counselling philosophy

At first glance, the philosophy that underpins the person-centred approach may seem universal. However, if we look at some of the values (see below) that underpin this philosophy, one can clearly see that they are not shared by all communities.

- Expressing your emotions with a stranger can be a good thing.
- Separating from parental/family influence is something to be aimed for.
- We have freedom of choice.
- Hierarchical structures are oppressive (Costa, 2002; Laungani, 1999).

These are often not the values held by the clients we work with, and may lead us into therapeutic consequences for clients that are other than we intend (Kearney, 1996).

Other writers, such as Laungani (1999) and Eleftheriadou (1994) discuss cross-cultural counselling models which challenge us to re-think assumptions about the values and beliefs we may think we share with our clients.

Agger (2001) shows that even interventions that may be appropriate for people from one culture may not be applied universally across ages, genders, or, in the following example, class. In the following example, the writer has been discussing the knitting circle set up as a psychosocial intervention for traumatized women in the former Yugoslavia.

The knitting circle in Croatia

After many talks with the women who participated in the pro-ject, the international NGO staff had realized that sitting in a circle and knitting and drinking coffee was an old peasant tradition among women from the region. It was a "self-healing" circle that had been practised for centuries during all the former wars and hardships people had gone through. By distributing wool and supplying coffee they were setting the scene for a communal prac-tice to develop among these refugee women, who often did not know each other, and needed new social networks. However, this would not have been the optimal approach among middle-class women in large cities, where psychotherapy was a normal activity that had been financed by the health system during the socialist government.

The learning from this example is that there is no standard cross-cultural counselling model. What is important is to be genuinely interested and concerned in trying to understand the worldview of the person in front of you and to make use of differ-ent methods of working that can help you to do just that.

One can see from the above example that not all groups share Western values (such as those listed on p. 130).

The adjustments that people have to make when they are moving between cultures include finding a way to respond to new values that underpin the culture they are moving to. This can cause a kind of stress referred to as acculturation stress (Eleftheriadou, 1994). All of our clients have to make these adjustments.

A framework that helps us to attend to the way in which people adapt to living in new cultures and the stresses this can cause is Berry's (1990) model of acculturation. This helps to explain the way in which negotiating one's way between more than one culture can play itself out. Berry suggests that there are four ways in which we make these adjustments: separation, assimilation, marginalization, or integration.

In order to assess which of these four ways is the organizing principle for a person, two questions can be asked:

1. Is it considered to be of value to maintain one's original and inherited cultural identity and characteristics?
2. Is it considered to be of value to maintain relationships with other groups in one's environment?

    If the answer is yes to questions 1 and 2, the organizing principle is that of integration.

    If the answer is yes to question 1 and no to question 2, the organizing principle is that of separation.

    If the answer is no to question 1 and yes to question 2, the organizing principle is that of assimilation.

    If the answers are no to question 1 and 2, the organizing principle is that of marginalization.

One of the main purposes of cross-cultural therapy is to help individuals to integrate into society. If this is the case, it is clear that to be able to operate within and beyond familiar cultural parameters is necessary. This can frequently be a highly demanding process for people, where certainties may be called into question and new roles tried out. Therefore, we try to bear in mind the way in which individuals are negotiating their way through this adjustment. The following gives a case example of work with a client who presented as "marginalized".

Lena

Lena, a young woman of South Asian origin, had been born and brought up in Britain. She had been referred to the service as she had been self-harming. She presented with feelings of isolation and self-loathing. She was self-harming and had an eating disorder. She was constantly questioning her identity and sense of belonging. She rejected her South Asian origins and felt she did not fit in with British culture. She felt marginalized (Berry, 1990), unsafe, and cut off from everything and everyone.

She felt that not wearing South Asian dress or attending family religious festivals was a very clear communication about what she did not want to be associated with. She was clear that she did not want to see a South Asian counsellor. This seemed to be entirely consistent with her experience of marginalization and the counsellor deemed it as unhelpful at this stage to do little more than express mild curiosity about this request. The client expressed concern about being judged. At this stage in the relationship, this was not challenged further, but provided helpful information for the counsellor about the client's sense of herself and rejection of anything connected with her cultural identity. Indeed, Lena seemed to be very anxious about being overwhelmed and consumed by her culture of origin unless she held it firmly at bay.

It was not until Lena had allowed herself to speak of the racism she had experienced at school that she was able to make links with how she now felt about her own family. She made links between this experience and the shame she felt about her family's cultural heritage. A belief had grown in her that she needed to distance herself from her family's origins, culture, religion, etc. This, however, brought her little comfort, as she did not feel she belonged to the predominant mainstream culture either.

Her sense of isolation, exclusion, and self-hatred had intensified, and she had found herself feeling either excluded or being overwhelmed by the cultures around her. Once this had been expressed, Lena agreed to try out some experiments in order to start to move away from the polarized position of marginalization she had become frozen into. She agreed to try to do some research around one aspect of her religion at the library and feed back about it at the following session. During the week, although this was quite a strange experience for her, she found she was able to do this and not to feel overwhelmed by it. She also noticed that she was finding things a little easier at home, and that she was not rejecting everything as she had been previously.

She was beginning to negotiate a path between different cultures and to find her own way. This was now becoming a creative, enriching, and life-affirming experience. She had stopped self-harming and had not binged on food for the previous month. By the end of the counselling, she was able to communicate better with her family and to hear their views without feeling overwhelmed; she was able to hear feedback from her tutor at college as positive feedback and not as judging criticism, and she was able to take part in a religious festival with her family without feeling that she would become swamped by it. She was beginning to think that maybe her family's background could be a source of pride and belonging rather than of shame. The counsellor had modelled a self-assuredness in her own background throughout the sessions. This, perhaps, had contributed to the client's shift in attitude towards her own background. Her parting gift was a card she had made herself with a picture of a vibrant, luxuriant flower on the front, which she intended to nurture, sustain, and develop.

As shown by the above case study, marginalization is the rejection of one's own culture and the culture of other groups. It is often very difficult to form a therapeutic alliance with people who present with this. In this particular case, the nature of the counselling service offered at Mothertongue helped the client to develop some trust, perhaps precisely because the service is not aligned to any specific culture. It describes itself as a "multi-ethnic counselling service". This may have provided Lena with a safe space in which to work, a "transitional cultural space" (see Chapter Six for explanation) for the time needed to explore the issues in safety. In this example, the transitional cultural space may have allowed the client to voice experiences of racism.

Adapting a client-led model

We recognize that many of our clients will find it dificult to engage with a purely explorative therapeutic space. We try, therefore, to be flexible in our approach and incorporate a psycho-educational model, which includes the imparting of information and models which attempt to explain some aspects of human behaviour and interaction.

For some of our clients, not only is the concept of counselling unfamiliar, but also the notion of client-led care or education. It can be difficult for clients to engage with counselling, if, especially in the early stages, there is no discernible input from the counsellor.

For some clients, they will need to see that the counsellor has something to offer them in order to be able to trust that he or she is a valid professional. Although advice or guidance is not offered, it may be appropriate to offer more in the form of information and skills sharing. However, it is important to add a note of caution here. As with any guidelines, it is always important to consider the appropriacy of their application in different contexts. Personally, I am aware of having wanted to reach for any structural input out of a sense of desperation when listening to someone's harrowing story of loss and destruction. The feelings elicited in me as a bystander can seem so unbearable that I feel tempted to do anything to move us both away from them (see Eleftheriadou, Chapter Ten). But it may be at a moment like this that I am being called upon specifically to bear witness to the depth of the pain that my client has to endure. The following case example may illustrate this further.

Sara

A young woman, called Sara, an asylum seeker from Burundi, came to see me for counselling. She had lost her mother, relatives, and friends when she was forced to flee her country aged fifteen and come to this country to seek asylum.

Over the weeks she attended counselling she had brought her inconsolable grief to the sessions, sometimes speaking in English and sometimes speaking in her own language (which I did not speak). She talked about how she wanted to move on from this grief, to cut off from her past and to start again as if this were a completely new life in a new country. Although we were able to give her practical support through our support programme to get housing and training and employment, this only afforded her very limited relief. I felt lost in her grief, unable to understand the communication some of the time as it was in another language. There were various interpretations I could have made about the countertransferential feelings of loss and confusion, but I wish to focus on the struggle not to act upon my feelings of inadequacy and my sense of uselessness.

Together we seemed trapped by her past. In one session, she described a vivid dream where she was trying to crawl along like a baby. She was wearing a long black dress that kept trammelling up underneath her, impeding her progress. She described it graphically and I could imagine myself caught up in the folds of the dress. She herself made links between this dream and her own halting and hesitant attempts to engage with her future. It was difficult for me to hold on to the therapeutic role of container for these frustrations. With the help of supervision and by role reversing, in my imagination, with Sara, I was able to find a way to tolerate witnessing the profound sense of loss and devastation until eventually, Sara had a new dream, which heralded a turning point in the therapy.

She dreamed that she met a deeply religious man from her country who was holding and reading three Holy Books simultaneously. When she asked him if she could learn to do that, he replied, "No." When she asked why not, he replied, "First, you have to know what you have." On recounting this dream, its significance was startling to her. It had an immediate impact on her life and it helped her to take stock. She had been trying to sever connections with her past life from before she came to the UK and she now became able to make a link with the past again and allow it to co-exist with her present, as well as to plan for the future. She was able to value what she had achieved since she had arrived in the UK, and to recognize how she had kept her faith in God. This had been of great significance to her throughout her life, and she felt that it had been further deepened and strengthened. Since recounting this dream, Sara has been able to establish herself in a flat, is no longer in receipt of benefits, but is employed in a job she enjoys and is undertaking vocational training. Staying with her frustrations and bearing witness to her anguish helped her to find a way forward.

The wider social frame

The community development approach

Community development is a way of working that leads to the development of "active and sustainable communities based on social justice and mutual respect" (Barr & Hashagen, 2000). It does not have a definitive set of tools or activities, but works to strengthen people's skills and to remove barriers that prevent people from participating in, influencing, and making decisions about, issues that affect their lives. The following model (Figure 1) may help to illustrate this.

At the heart of the ABCD approach is the idea of community empowerment, described as a "core purpose" of community development, the other core purpose being to gain improvement in the quality of community life.

As referred to earlier in this chapter, the Mothertongue Counselling Service is located within a broader community service. The counselling service has not been able to sit and wait for clients independently coming to seek help with mental health issues, because they generally do not for a number of reasons, which include:

- lack of trust in services and a sense of having been let down in the past;

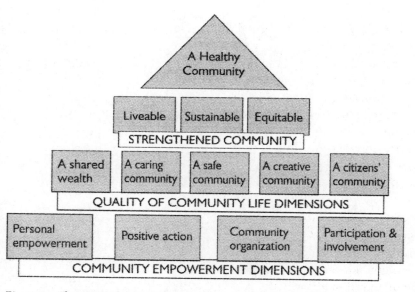

Figure 1. The ABCD (Achieving Better Community Development) Framework evaluating community development interventions (Barr & Hashagen, 2000).

- the stigma associated with mental health issues;
- barriers to accessing services, such as problems with transport or childcare that need to be addressed;
- people from BME communities often consider their practical and social needs to be more pressing than emotional or mental health needs;
- the need to communicate in a language other than English.

In an attempt to address some of these problems, Mothertongue has needed to engage actively with communities in order to deliver information verbally, often approaching issues of mental health in an oblique fashion through "community engagement and mental health promotion activities", for example, cultural activities, information sharing, general information-giving sessions, and general mental health awareness and information. Although this can be time consuming, it has proved essential to build up relationships and trust at grass roots level. It has also been extremely useful to form professional relationships with health and social care professionals who are already trusted within the community. They are able to make "collaborative referrals" into the service. It has been imperative to be able to help people get assistance with their practical problems from within the service, so we have developed a "Cross-cultural Support Project".

There has been a need to build the capacity of the service to deal with the work that the project generates. For this reason, it has been essential to the work of the service to include a training component to build up a trained workforce that is representative both in ethnicity and in languages spoken. Finally, the service has found ways of helping people to voice their concerns and to participate in influencing the way in which services are delivered in future, so that their needs can be met.

Throughout, it has been crucial to be delivering on all of these through action and not just through consultation. It seems that trust is built on the changes that people can see taking place, rather than focus groups and the contributions they may make to developing strategies. All of these activities fit within the "Community Empowerment Dimensions" level of the ABCD model outlined in Figure 1, and are illustrated in Figure 2.

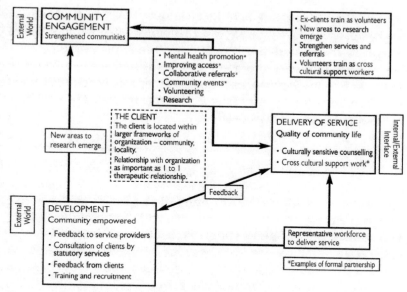

Figure 2. The Mothertongue Counselling Service model.

Community engagement

We are aware that to engage with some ethnic minority groups, we need to be outreaching into communities and meeting them where they are. The process of counselling needs to be dynamic and interactive. We need to be able to give information and explain about what we do. Therefore, we put on a range of community activities, such as sari tying demonstrations, hand massage, and yoga sessions, where we are able to promote and explain the service and to engage with people who would otherwise not engage with the service at all.

We have also been able to gain access to communities and to engage with and involve communities in the planning and delivery of counselling and mental health related activities by means of our volunteering programme. By offering a professional training course in cross-cultural support, we have attracted people from BME communities to volunteer with the service. For some, it may offer the pathway to employment; for others, it may offer a way of contributing to their communities. Once they are engaged with the organization in this way, they frequently make use of the services we offer. Some may seek help for themselves. Although they may not have approached us initially for help, it is often felt to be more acceptable to approach a service offering, rather than seeking, help. This makes the work more complex and requires our constant attention to boundary issues. Some volunteers may refer clients to us, others have joined our Management Committee. All contribute to the running of the organization.

Mental health promotion and research

By carrying out mental health promotional events and research projects, we are able to make contact with communities and to make ourselves visible to people who might otherwise have no knowledge of the service. As a result of our work with clients, we are able to identify gaps in service provision and future areas for research. The following example may serve to illustrate this.

Young asylum seeker leaflet project

Between October 2004 and March 2005, we created a project involving young volunteers aged between fourteen and nineteen who produced a stress management leaflet. This was translated into six different languages and was aimed at young asylum seekers. The aim was to engage them in the design and creation of a product and for their knowledge and skills to be used and valued. The project was set up by three organizations, in partnership, that have been working with young asylum seekers over a number of years: Mothertongue, Social Services Leaving Care Team, and Sasir, a local voluntary support service for asylum seekers in Reading.

Many of the young asylum seekers involved in the project have suffered traumatic experiences in their countries of origin and have a range of health problems. Some who have been in this country for years have no idea that they could get help or treatment for these problems. Until this leaflet was produced, there has been no other accessible information or help for this extremely vulnerable group locally. The leaflet gives information about how to access help and information about their symptoms of stress, and tips for alleviating or managing them. The project used a person-centred approach by conducting interviews with young asylum seekers to find out about their experiences and what information they would find useful to include in the leaflet. The asylum seekers helped to identify the most needed languages and were involved in translating, as well as participating in the steering group with advice on design, cultural input, content, and distribution.

The impact already seen is that people are able to access information in their own language and gain understanding of the forms and symptoms of stress and anxiety they experience in order to normalize what they often reported as frightening symptoms. A seventeen-year-old asylum seeker who worked on the project described the experience of leaving their home country and coming to a new country as "being like a blind person that can see nothing or do nothing without help". For the young people producing the leaflet, it has been a very productive experience. They have learnt about the process of leaflet production and they have also made real contact for the first time with young asylum seekers from eight different countries. Clients using the leaflet have reported the following:

> "It is so good to see something like this in my own language";

> "It made me laugh when my counsellor tried to say some of the words in my language and that is when I started to feel at ease with her";

> "I understand why I am feeling like this and that has helped me";

> "The breathing exercises help. I read through the tips when I am feeling stressed";

> "I am trying to take more exercise now I understand how it can help me";

> "It feels good that someone has bothered to produce this for us".

By providing this basic information in Albanian, Arabic, English, Farsi, French, and Swahili, more people can be reached initially in a cost-effective way, without having to use individual interpreters. As a result of this, we have also seen a significant increase in the number of young asylum seekers referred to, and accessing, our services.

Collaborative referrals

For many of our counselling clients, our initial engagement with them involves establishing a pre-counselling relationship. Accessing any form of mental health support may be very difficult for some clients, who may fear being labelled as "mad". Psychological problems are a stigma and are often kept hidden within the family in home countries. Relying only on clients referring themselves will discriminate against those who may have no concept of counselling, who may fear being misunderstood linguistically, culturally, or both, or who may lack the confidence or the experience of exercising their own choice and autonomy with regard to their treatment. It has been vital to the success of the service to build up a relationship with referrers, such as Health Visitors, GPs, and teachers, among many, who are already trusted by their clients. The referrers work together with us collaboratively by encouraging and referring clients into the service and by bridging the path between the referrer and the counselling service.

Once someone is referred, we normally make the first telephone contact with the client in the client's preferred language. This is particularly useful for people who may have little or no money to make a telephone call, who may be anxious about having to speak English on the telephone, or who may need encouragement to try an initial session.

Cross-cultural Support Project

For many of our clients, emotional distress is often tied up with practical problems. Tidyman (2004) identifies risk factors for mental health deterioration. These include: family living arrangements; having work that does not use people's qualifications; negative experiences of health services; the impact of cold weather. It has, therefore, been important to provide help from within the service with those aspects of the client's life through a team of trained cultural support volunteers and workers. This team is also able to help with form filling, accessing welfare benefits, attending professional appointments, advocacy, confidence building, and supporting independence. Counsellors can refer into our own project so that clients continue to access help within the service while maintaining their therapeutic boundary, as the following description of one case illustrates.

Hannah

Hannah was receiving counselling from Mothertongue. During the counselling, she revealed that she had no way of paying for the NHS spectacles she had been prescribed. She had been in receipt of The National Asylum Support Service (NASS) vouchers and had no recourse to cash. Although the client was finding the counselling beneficial, it was clear that her most basic needs were not being met. The counsellor was able to maintain therapeutic boundaries by referring this client to the cross-cultural support service. They were able to locate a small local trust fund that was able to pay the balance for the spectacles. Not to have been able to help with this may have rendered the counselling irrelevant and out of touch.

Providing this broad and holistic service is particularly relevant for the client group with whom we work. Asylum seekers and refugees may have experienced the whole or partial destruction of their communities or ethnic groups. Schlapobersky suggests,

> Separate individual treatments and discrete unrelated resources are less useful than the resources of a team. Survivors' feelings of grief, rage and helplessness need a containing environment where staff can accept and work with them ... Survivors need a relationship with a community rather than with a specific treatment ... [1993, p. 5]

Our clients, who may or may not come from a refugee background, may experience their patterns of attachment more profoundly with a group, for example, the family, extended family, or community, than with an individual. Clients at Mothertongue may feel a strong sense of attachment to their individual counsellor or support worker, but we have found that their attachment to Mothertongue as an organization is also of great importance to them.

Clients frequently return to the service as volunteers. There are a number of ways in which volunteers offer their services, from fundraising to supporting and providing advocacy for clients. In our initial training of volunteers, we are able to assess the level of involvement and type of work it is appropriate for people to take on. This is monitored through ongoing supervision. We use only professionally qualified, paid counsellors for clinical work. We fund a scheme for a selection of our volunteers to train to become counsellors. For many of the people who volunteer with us, it is part of the creative cycle of healing and the wish to be of use to others. This, in turn, mirrors the cycle of life in extended families and communities, where people move in and out of roles of dependency and leadership during different stages of their life cycle.

Training component

The *National Service Framework* (Department of Health, 1999) highlights various issues in relation to ethnic minorities and mental health. One of these is that the recruitment of local staff from the particular ethnic communities is the most effective longer-term strategy in making services more attractive to ethnic minorities.

It quickly became clear to us that there was a gap in a trained workforce representative of the diverse communities we sought to serve.

It is often tempting to recruit someone because they speak an appropriate language, but who may not have the training and experience required for the task. Many of the professional roles in the area of health and social care require very high levels of understanding and experience of professional behaviour, and, in many ways, the most basic support and care roles are often the most demanding in terms of behaving with professionalism and compassion while distinguishing between a work and a social role.

Our training includes initial and ongoing training and supervision for our Cultural Support Volunteers, and an initiative in partnership with the Berkshire Department of Clinical Psychology and Berkshire Healthcare NHS Trust to offer innovative training in intercultural therapy—"Advanced training in Culturally Sensitive Practice".

As a service committed to the community development model, we respond to the needs we see presenting around us in the community. One of our most recent projects has addressed the need mental health professionals have expressed for interpreters who understand how to work in a mental health context. Consequently, we have created a training DVD which illustrates a collaborative model of mental health clinicians and interpreters working together. We have also established a dedicated pool of interpreters, which we make available to the local Primary Care Trust, who are trained in this method and who have an understanding of:

- mental health issues and terminology;
- the ways of working therapeutically as a triad rather than as a dyad;
- the extent, limitations, and professional boundaries of their role;
- the nature of therapeutic change;
- their relationship with the mental health professional.

Another project has developed as a response to concerns parents expressed to us about communicating with their teenage children during the making of a DVD called *My Life*. In this DVD, a group of first, second, and third generation BME young people and older BME people are invited to talk about the experiences of young people growing up in today's multi-cultural Britain: how they experience themselves, and how other people experience them, and what they believe are the issues facing first, second, and third generation BME young people in the UK today.

We wanted to respond actively to the parents' concerns. We have always found that, rather than doing extensive consultations with our clients at Mothertongue, it is better to set up a pilot and test responses to the pilot. In that way, our clients receive something and then can comment about it, rather than having to imagine what they might want without any shaping of expectations.

We have, therefore, trained our counsellors to facilitate the cross-cultural parent groups with the purpose of helping participants to rediscover a good model of communication between generations for their own families, while considering the effects of changing cultures and migration on family life.

Services for BME communities have tended to develop in an *ad hoc* fashion, without sufficient infrastructure and strategic vision, in the voluntary sector. The commitment to training people from BME communities to take on professional roles in health and social care means that consistent and sustained development of appropriate services can occur.

Conclusion

I have attempted to demonstrate the way in which a culturally sensitive counselling service can engage with BME communities, some of whom have traditionally been regarded as hard to reach. The model suggested creates a bridge between the clinical and community development work, and forms a three-stage interactive model. From the experiences gained by working with clients in a support or advocacy role, it often becomes clear that there is a broader role that we can play within the context of statutory service provision. Service providers are keen to capitalize on the relationship of trust that we have established with our clients and seek to link with our clients in order to consult with them on service satisfaction, development, and provision. We also gain insight into some of the endemic problems experienced by clients attempting to access services, and increasingly we are able to use that insight to help service providers to think about ways in which they may need to improve their services so that they are more relevant for clients from BME communities.

References

Agger, I. (2001). The problem of the wool: a response (Section 4). In: M. Loughry & A. Ager (Eds.), *Refugee Studies Centre Refugee Experience—Psychosocial Training Module*. Oxford: Refugee Studies Centre (online resource). http://earlybird.qeh.ox.ac.uk/rfgexp/rsp_tre/student/wool/toc.htm

Barr, A., & Hashagen, S. (2000). *Achieving Better Community Development ABCD Framework Handbook: A Framework for Evaluating Community Development*. London: Community Development Foundation.

Berry, J. W. (1990). *Psychology of Acculturation: Understanding Individuals Moving Between Cultures*. London: Sage.

British Psychodrama Association, Cross Cultural and Equality Consultative Committee (2003). *Handbook for Psychodramatists and Sociodramatists Part one: Race, Ethnicity and Culture*.

Costa, B. (2002). Psychodrama across cultures. *British Journal of Psychodrama and Sociodrama*, 17: 37–47.

Department of Health (1999). *National Service Framework for Mental Health: Modern Standards and Service Model*. London: Crown Copyright.

Eleftheriadou, Z. (1994). *Transcultural Counselling*. London: Central Books.

Fox, A. (2001). An interpreter's perspective. *Context*, 54: 19–20.

Kearney, A. (1996). *Counselling, Class and Politics; Undeclared Influences in Therapy*. Ross on Wye: PCCS Books.

Laungani, P. (1999). Culture and identity: implications for counselling. In: S. Palmer & P. Laungani (Eds.), *Counselling in a Multicultural Society* (pp. 35–70). London: Sage.

Rogers, C. (1951). *Client-centred Therapy*. London: Constable.

Schlapobersky, J. (1993). The reclamation of space and time: a political application of psychotherapy. Unpublished, presented at The Political Psyche, Institute of Contemporary Arts, London, 27 November.

Shaikh, Z. (1999). *Between Two Cultures*. London: EACH.

The New Shorter Oxford English Dictionary (1993). Vol. 1. Oxford: Oxford University Press.

Tidyman, M. (2004). Making it diverse. In: *Radical Mentalities Briefing Paper 3*. London: Sainsbury Centre for Mental Health.

Tribe, R., & Raval, H. (2003). *Working with Interpreters in Mental Health*. London: Brunner-Routledge.

CHAPTER NINE

The stories of four Bosnian women

Edina Dzeko

Introduction

We have seen and witnessed many wars and political conflicts in recent history. The war in Bosnia broke out in April 1992, after the country's independence from the former Yugoslavia. Over many centuries, different ethnic groups lived in harmony, sharing their religious beliefs. This was the nature of the country that people were most proud of. Mosques, synagogues, Catholic and Orthodox churches have been the symbol of Bosnia as well as the presence of Gypsy/Roma people. This tranquillity changed when the war from neighbouring countries came to Bosnia. The phrases such as ethnic cleansing, genocide, concentration camps, mass graves, all happening in the middle of Europe, became Bosnia's everyday reality that the world watched on television screens. Sarajevo, the capital, was under the siege, the longest lasting siege since the Middle Ages. Most cultural and religious institutions across the country were destroyed. The extent of this war was directly reflected in the number of Bosnian refugees worldwide.

Refugees and living in exile

The term refugee refers to people who have had to leave their country because of violence and repression or wars. They reach the country of exile searching for safety. Each refugee has an individual and unique story of his or her own to tell. They all try to adjust to the new environment, which depends on many factors, such as age, personal experiences, family situation, and motivation, among others. Refugees have to live with loss of status, culture shock, and the attitude of the host country. This process of adjusting and integrating is very complex. They are in situations where they face new social and cultural conditions which are different to those in their own countries, and these cultural differences may make refugees feel isolated and confused (van der Veer, 1998).

Talking about refugees and their experiences in exile, however, cannot be generalized. It should be seen according to their own individual way of experiencing the new country. Some refugees described living in exile as a positive experience, where they tried to rebuild their lives in spite of all difficulties (Summerfield, 1999). Therefore, the important point to consider is how refugees manage to rebuild their lives and what the experiences of being refugees mean to them.

Counselling and refugees

Counselling and psychotherapy are very common in the West, and individuals are used to these ideas from an early age. However, many refugees come from a cultural background in which talking to outsiders about their experiences or emotional difficulties is just not done, and the fact that many refugees do not seek help does not mean that some of them do not need it (van der Veer, 1998). They usually believe that counselling and psychology services offered in the West would not be beneficial for them. Most refugees come from countries where counselling, as a profession, does not exist, and everyday problems would be discussed with friends and relatives. Counselling as a profession did not exist in Bosnia until professionals from the West introduced it during the war (Giller, 1998).

Richman (1998) states that supporting refugees is not simply a question of treating their trauma. It requires an understanding of the complexity of their situation and the adaptation they must make living in exile. Many refugees avoid feeling overwhelmed by devoting their energy to the most urgent practical considerations. Emotions about loss and separation are controlled in order to manage what is most pressing. Similarly, van der Veer (1998) writes that the models which have been developed in working with refugees are mainly concerned with clinical and medical symptoms.

When working with refugees, Summerfield (1995) draws attention to the importance of rebuilding a network for mutual social support, strengthening the family and community structures. Often, individuals who have been through traumatic experiences feel they want to talk about their experiences in an emotionally supportive environment. This includes their preferences for talking to people in the same social network who have had similar experiences.

Most refugees seem to demonstrate their ability to adapt to the demands of the new environment. This may vary from individual to individual. They would also adapt various strategies to survive, depending on their individual strengths and the strengths of their community network. By recognizing refugees' personal experiences and the meanings they address to them, the focus of working with refugees is on seeing individuals in relationship to others and the culture they come from.

Background to the study

The following account is part of a study that was based on using semi-structured interviews and qualitative analysis. The aim was to gain a picture of the participants' experiences of being refugees. In this way, the participants were seen as experts on the topic. The term "refugee" was used to describe these women who had to leave Bosnia due to war, rather than whether they had been granted full refugee status. Also, the term "exile" was used to refer to the participant being in the host country and essentially unable to return, rather than whether they had been expelled or had willingly left their native country. The interview questions had primary emphasis on inviting the participants to reflect upon their experiences of being refugees, and how they perceived counselling as professional help. The questions asked are shown below.

- If you experienced any difficulties, who would you have talked to?
- If you asked for help, what type of help did you hope to get?
- Have you felt you wanted to integrate to the new culture or keep with your own culture?
- Have you tried to make friends with people who had the same experience as you or people who had a different experience from you?
- What was the most helpful thing you received from people who offered you help?
- What kept you going during difficult time?
- Have you felt your life had a meaning at the time?
- Have you been offered counselling, and did you have a notion of what counselling is in the West?
- How did you feel when you received news from home?
- Have you felt people were asking you personal questions that you did not want to answer?
- How would you describe your journey of being a refugee, what did it meant to you to be a refugee?
- Where is home?

Participants

Five Bosnian women refugees agreed to take part in the study, four gave permission for their stories to be published. As I am from this background myself, it was not difficult to find participants for the study within the Bosnian community. I told friends and acquaintances about the need to interview refugee women about their experiences of living in exile and asked them to spread the word. I was seeking to interview refugee women, as it was likely that Bosnian women would be more approachable than men in this context. Prior to interviews, they were informed that they could disclose as much or as little personal information as they felt was appropriate for them. They all reported memories of their personal journeys of being refugees, as well as their own coping mechanisms of adjusting to the new way of life in England. The following seven themes emerged from the text.

Who is the counselling for?

Most refugees come from the countries where counselling as a profession did not exist, and their knowledge and understanding of this profession was in accordance with traditional medical views of mental health. The approaches developed in the West for treatment of refugees emphasize the need for counselling, due to the traumatic events they have undergone. In this study, refugees were asked about what they thought of counselling and whether they felt they needed such professional help. The following extracts from the text describe their attitude towards counselling. They stated how unfamiliar they were with mental health services as they exist in the UK. Their concept of counselling was highly stigmatized by their previous conceptions of mental health in their country. However, they also stated that after a few years of living in the UK, their perceptions have changed.

> I never had counselling in my country and didn't have any expectations of counselling here. I don't, I cannot say that I really knew what it was. In the beginning I thought it was a waste of time; but after a few years of being here, after a while, I accepted it.

> It's probably when you talk to a third person who helps you open up and say things you wouldn't say to other people. I think that helps, that everyone needs counselling and that does not mean you are mad, that is not just if you are mad. I think this now, but this is not what I was thinking eight years ago. Then I thought you needed counselling only if you are down and you are on Prozac, if you are mad, a bit crazy and you need professional help. That's what I was thinking then, but I have a bit wider opinion about it now (laughs).

The presented view is in accordance with the traditional view they held about mental health, as it was perceived in their own country. The second indicates an awareness of talking to a "third party". Although at first she believed she did not belong to the group of people needing counselling, after a few years she perceived counselling as a profession helping people with their everyday difficulties. The interesting point to note is they both laughed as they were talking about their new opinions of counselling. Although it is often said that laughter is a defence against painful feelings, I experienced their laughter as a way of expressing their awareness of how much they have changed and were able to reflect on the attitudes and beliefs they used to hold. Following from this, another extract from the text shows a similar attitude.

> I have grown to realize what counselling is. I didn't think at the time I needed it, counselling or therapy of any sort; but at the same time I didn't realize the difference between counselling here and anywhere else. Again it goes back to what I said; I wanted to be treated as normal, not to be seen as a clinical case; and my understanding, umm, thinking that I didn't need it at the time—maybe, maybe later.

The remark "clinical case" perhaps suggests her fear of being labelled and seen as a psychiatric case. However, like the previous two participants, she did not exclude the possibility of having counselling at a later stage in her life, when she would have had a different understanding of counselling and would have felt at ease to enter into a therapeutic relationship. Blackwell (2005, p. 18) suggests that many people manage without such treatments and that "having counselling or psychotherapy is a subjective existential choice". Similarly, Thomas (2007) points out that not everyone who is referred for therapy will need it. This is reflected in the following extract:

> I have been offered counselling, but I didn't have a notion of what it is. I survived the worst things in my life by putting them in writing and that is kind of cleansing for me, instead of talking to someone. I did it in writing and that helped me a lot in Sarajevo and I continued to do the same here. I just didn't see it at the time; that would help me that I would go to someone and talk about what had happened. I don't, I didn't see the meaning; still wouldn't.

For this participant counselling had no meaning at the time she arrived in England and it had no meaning at the time of conducting the interviews. She described that writing was her way of dealing with the difficult time during the war in Sarajevo. She did not deny having experienced a difficult time; however, she did not feel that the offered counselling would be the way she could express herself. She found her own way of dealing with her difficulties; the way that she believed was most beneficial for her. Ehrenberg (2007) gives a moving account. Although not a refugee himself, but descended from a family who suffered persecution, he describes how he became a psychoanalyst, stating that writing helped him deal with day to day problems.

Can you understand my story?

This theme describes how these four refugees wanted to talk about their feelings, but in attempting to do so they felt misunderstood. Consequently, they thought they could not talk to people in the host country.

> I went through a lot in Sarajevo, and here as well. I spent two and a half years during the war there; the worst years and I thought no one could actually understand. If I speak to someone, no one would understand; it's normal, we have the thing in our country saying "sit gladnom ne vjeruje". You can translate it for your research and I think it's true.

Here, the participant compared her memories of, and feelings about, the war in Sarajevo to those of living in exile. The phrase she used in Bosnian means: if you have a full stomach, you cannot understand the one who is starving. She assumed that the people in the host country have not had similar experiences, and hence they could not understand what it would be like to be in a war. It is true that for the majority of people in the West, the reality of war is a distant concept.

> I think for some people there is no need explaining the situation because they are confused and I understand that. It is a bit confusing. If you say you are from Bosnia and Sarajevo, they always think you are this and that, they can't really understand. I try not to talk about it any more.

People were asking questions because they didn't know and some-how they seemed personal questions. But it's, I know now, because they don't know, they don't have a clue what they were talking about or asking about. Yea, some people were curious and they liked to ask a lot. Uh, very often I feel, even if I answer on that question, you are not going to understand.

These refugees believed people could not understand them even if they answered their questions. The feeling of not being heard and listened to contributed to their decision to stop talking about themselves and their circumstances. This helped them protect themselves from further pain of being misunderstood. Van der Veer (1998) explains that the feeling of not being understood is not a surprise, since refugees come from different cultural norms and backgrounds, which at times can be seen as backward, according to western norms.

What is our priority?

The interviewed refugees were asked what type of help they needed. They all stated that practical help was their main priority. In their opinion, things such as getting a flat, being able to study at university, getting advice on housing and immigration issues were what they felt they needed at the time. Seeking emotional support had little or no importance for them. It is often said that refugees need emotional help to overcome their traumatic experiences; however, the same view was not shared by these refugees.

Practical help, yes, I needed in the beginning. Practical help in a way what my rights are, what I can do; do I have let's say national health; then people from university, schools, how to get classes without paying for them, and many other things like that.

Most of the institutions if I may call them like that, they were really helpful, even though you have to wait for a long time to get things and you have to fill in many application forms—I found them help-ful. Especially institutions like education, that they are doing special thing for refugees. Umm, for me personally, council as well, because I got a council flat and I think they were very helpful.

Getting a council flat was one of the most helpful things for me and
I appreciate it a lot.

The extracts from the text show that their priority was to deal
with practical issues. They described how having these needs met
was extremely helpful for them. They initially needed this help,
which enabled them to help themselves later. Loizos (2002) has
emphasized that refugees need to be encouraged to voice their
opinion regarding what type of help they would find most useful.

If I asked for help, oh, that was probably housing problems or
income problems or it was basically all the problems we were going
through. It was the situation with flats, it's basically just normal,
everyday problems we were going through; just like settling.

I needed money for a flat, which was one of the things I needed so
badly; so that was something I would never forget. People who
gave us a flat we have now, it's housing association people, so that
was the time when we needed help.

The participants described what type of help they needed as
refugees, and talked about "everyday problems" and how they felt
settled once they had a place to live. They did not talk about their
emotions at the time, if they felt overwhelmed with the life changes.
The help they needed was not any form of therapy or talking about
their problems. They wanted to have a place to live as this gave
them a sense of security. Being refugees who had lost almost everything, all they wanted was to feel settled and to continue their lives
in exile. Papadopoulos (2002) writes about what it means for a
refugee to lose his home and that it is the loss of home which is the
only condition all refugees share, not trauma. Understandably, once
they reach exile, refugees want to have a place they could call home.

Mainly I wanted to get help with bureaucratic things, mainly how
does the system works, how can I get a flat, how can I go to university, and who can I talk about practical issues.

The interviewed refugees gave their personal experiences of the
help they received and how it enabled them to re-start their lives.
This theme is consistent with the findings of Giller (1998) and

Richters (1998), who carried out the trauma workshops in Sarajevo and Uganda. They set up projects which provided professional help, such as counselling and medical advice, but refugees who came for help asked for money and housing. They felt that the war was over and therefore their problems had been to rebuild their homes and lives on a more practical level. Therefore, when working with refugees, it is important to listen to them and the needs they believe would be most appropriate for them. Summerfield (1996) says that the direction of survivors' concerns is not inwards, towards their emotional lives, but outwards, towards their shattered social world.

The search for meaning

On hearing the question, all the participants paused, they were in deep thought for a few moments and seemed to be lost for words. They described feeling some confusion and disbelief, as if they could not really believe what they had been through. In reflecting upon their experiences, they stated that having a meaning in their lives, having something to hold on to gave them strength to cope with their lives in England. They talked about how crucial it was to believe, to hope for a better future.

> Probably thinking that I am still young and that whatever I lost, everything my parents lost, that I am going to make up for everything, try to rebuild, carry on living. It was mostly positive thinking; I was never really going down. I have never seen it as there is no end, there is no better life. I was always hoping something was going to happen.

For this refugee positive thinking and hope for a better life gave her the strength. This optimism may be an individual personality trait, but in a similar way, another refugee stated that she wanted to have a normal life, which she described as follows.

> Uh, what was the meaning to me, umm? To have a normal life. I think I said it before, a struggle towards a normal life. It all felt temporary. I felt there was going to be an end to it, so it felt temporary.

Here, the text shows how the wish and hope to end the "struggle" helped this refugee cope with the changes in her life at the time. It gave her a sense of meaning. She felt that the initial years were not "normal life" and the belief that it would come to an end helpful. The term "normal" had a personal meaning to her, and this study was focusing on how something was subjectively experienced by the refugee herself. She constructed her own reality and gave it her own meaning. In other words, she saw her life as she experienced it.

> I always wanted to be happy, and I was trying to do so even though it was really difficult. But I just wanted to be normal, young woman. Oh, this is really deep (laughs). I don't know what to say. I just wanted to settle down and to be able to call this place my home and what I was doing was building my home for me.

It was difficult for this refugee to think and reflect on her feelings on a deeper level. She did not know how she managed the difficult time in her life. Like the previous refugee, she also used the word "normal" while describing her life at the time. The opinion of Thomas (2007, p. 46) is that "being a refugee is not a normal part of life".

> What was the meaning? Well, I was happy that I survived. And I thought the things could only be better as the song says (sings a Bosnian song). I think once you are on the very bottom and you can't go further, you are down and you go up, down and up, and you are climbing up again. Every possible way, emotionally and any other aspect, I wanted to climb up.

This extract describes how this refugee was happy because she survived the war. In comparing life in exile with her earlier experiences, she thought that her life in exile could not be any worse than it was during the war. This is a very important point, as mentioned above. Many believe that refugees are traumatized because of the events they have gone through and, therefore, when they come to live in exile they need some professional help to overcome these difficulties. However, what is described here is that living in exile, reaching safety, helped this refugee feel settled and happy.

This theme described how important it is to have a meaning, belief, hope, or faith. Having a meaning encouraged these refugees to believe in themselves and a better life. They all gave their individual and unique meaning to their lives in the UK, how they perceived it and experienced it. They stated how they needed to regain a sense of direction in their lives and their personal values. They did not want to lose the sense of hope and a better future, they were aware that their world had been destroyed and it could never be the same again. However, this did not prevent them from searching for the new meanings in their lives.

Finding the positive in negative experience

Bracken, Giller, and Summerfield (1997) emphasized that refugees are seen as vulnerable individuals who have experienced trauma. Consequently, they are seen as victims in need of psychological help. Their experiences have been described as horrific and negative, but listening to the interviewed refugees in this study, it appears that they have managed to turn their negative experiences into positive ones. As Berry (1997) stated, forced migration does not necessarily lead to negative outcomes.

> All this is a journey. Journey, umm. I just wish that this journey was a bit shorter. It took a long time, it's a long journey and I hope that is an end of the same journey as well. But in general, I have been OK. I don't, it's hard to say it was a pleasant journey, but it was, it was. My best years, I have to say I learnt a lot, even though maybe I would do it somewhere else as well, but it happened to be here and it's OK. Its OK now, I smile now. I survived.

This participant had described that there were obstacles and difficulties she faced, but she managed to turn her experience into a positive one. The experience of being a refugee taught her a lot about herself and the world she lives in. There was some confusion in the way she spoke, indicating how difficult it was for her to reflect upon her experiences. She finished her sentence saying "I smile, I survived"—powerful words describing the depth of her feelings and experiences.

> It's a hell of a journey (laughing). I don't know how I can explain that, but it was a big experience and it's, it makes you understand

some things that I don't think you would. What we went through like nineteen, twenty-year-olds, not many teenagers went through the same we had to go through (pause). Umm, I can't explain it, it's, it's just make you, you grow up quickly than you would and it makes you quite stronger person as well.

Another refugee, in describing her experiences, appeared confused while talking about her struggle to overcome the obstacles she had to go through. She compared herself with people similar to her age. She had difficulties putting her feeling into words. She paused for a long time during her talk and she thought deeply about the question. What stands out is that her experience of being a refugee made her become a stronger person. The following shares her experience of shame.

Two things it meant. It made me ashamed many times, oh, possibly because I didn't want to discuss the details of it at all. Uh, many times really made me feel not entitled to many things; you are just not entitled to do this or that. On the other hand, I think it has been a great experience. It made me much stronger person and if I've gone through it, I could really do anything. It was positive and negative experience.

These interviewed refugees turned their experiences into personal success, giving their experiences personal and unique meanings. Of course, this theme cannot be generalized to the whole refugee population. It highlights how these four women refugees perceived themselves at that particular time in their lives. They did not accept the givens, but took responsibilities for being in such a difficult situation and tried to turn the given situation into something positive. Therefore, the importance of giving a meaning to a traumatic experience cannot be over-emphasized. In other words, these refugees did not see themselves as not being able to cope with the life changes, and, therefore, were able to relate to the new changes in their lives. Alayarian (2007) has written about refugees and their resilience to the traumatic experiences, and how, in spite of everything, they were able to find work, contribute, and integrate into the host country. She states that those refugees, among their other psychological makeup, thought positively, did not want to be seen as victims, and took responsibility for the difficult situation they were in.

Where do we belong?

During the interviews these women refugees described the difficulties of having to adjust to the new culture they were living in. They felt they wanted to keep aspects from their own culture, but also realized that the only way to live in the UK would be to integrate aspects of the host culture. Their aim was to find a balance between the two cultures. Initially, this process was difficult, because it seemed as if they were giving up their identities. They worked towards integrating and being part of the new society, which provided them with a sense of belonging to the new culture they were living in.

> I wanted to integrate, oh, yes. I wanted to integrate in the beginning, even now I do; but of course I wanted to keep something from my culture as well. I was trying to have both, like in parallel way. I have a feeling that I am OK, that I somehow have a balance here. And I am trying to accept the things I like from this culture and keep the ones from my culture that I think are right and I like them. So that's maybe a normal growing up process as well. I knew I was going to live here, if nothing just for few years and you just have to integrate. First of all language and be prepared to do things here.

This demonstrates how she was willing to adjust to the new environment and she saw herself as an individual, but also as a member of a larger society to which she wanted to belong. She had a need to be a part of the new culture, which she felt gave her the opportunity to rebuild her life.

> At the time I thought this was something new, this was something I liked, but you are somehow in between, you are losing a little bit of your culture, so it is a bit . . . I don't know . . . a bit confusing. I am more taking this culture as my own, but I don't take everything. There are things I would never understand about English culture, but there are some things that I adopted as well. So, it's a bit confusing (laughing).

In contrast to the previous participant, this refugee felt she was living in between two cultures rather than being part of both. She held on to some aspects of her cultural background, but there was confusion in describing this process of integration, as if she could not understand how this process took place. She does want to adopt certain aspects, but this demonstrates that integrating into a new society does not necessarily mean accepting everything, particularly things which are in contrast to an individual's belief system. Hence, this process of integration did not mean that she lost herself in the new culture.

> I was very keen to integrate into a new culture, because I thought if I am going to stay here for a long time and possibly for the rest of my life, I need to learn how this new culture works.

> Both, especially as I have a child on my own. I think it's important that I keep my own culture so he can understand better. I want him to know his origins, what his origins are, his background; I think that's important, but I also want him to be part of this country. This is the country where he is going to grow up and I think it will make him richer knowing two cultures. I was thirty-five when I came here, so I was pretty much established in my own culture, in my society. I had my place in it and it's not something you could just forget or disregard, but I also wanted to have both cultures.

Again there is a description of how these refugees wanted and needed to be part of the new culture. One of the women emphasized the importance of teaching her child about her background, a significant factor in forming the child's identity.

The stories of these refugee women were about learning to integrate, to belong to the new culture without being fearful of losing their own background. One could say they were young, and, therefore, the integration was a natural, growing-up process. One could also say that employing such a strategy to integrate made them feel part of the new culture, and this feeling of belonging encouraged them to rebuild their lives. Blackwell (2005) also observes this ability, reminding us that refugees are people with individual talents.

Denial or reality?

Following from the previous themes, this last theme emerged throughout the text as the interviewed refugees were describing their experiences. They stated that they were more concerned about resolving practical issues in their lives, whereas other issues were given less emphasis. It seems as if they had no time to think about them. This last theme describes their feelings regarding their loss. It describes their feelings about what they regarded as home— whether they considered the UK or Bosnia to be their home. This area, which had little attention before, has been explored by Papadopoulos (2002). Throughout the text, they stated how they had no time to think about their emotions, and how they just wanted to settle down and continue with their lives. One could say they were denying their feelings; that they were not in touch with the reality and the situation in which they were. Maybe they experienced their reality as so threatening that they shut themselves off in denial. Perhaps the fantasy of a better future served as a defence against the pain that would be experienced if they were to face everything they went through. One could, however, say that their feelings of being safe, secure, and settled in exile helped them deal with the past and they moved on. They all accepted it was difficult; however, they managed to live without any professional therapeutic help. They relied on their own coping strategies, which gave them strength and a belief in a better future. This was their reality.

> It's normal for human beings to forget, to try forget; you know bad things you experience, you just want to look forward to new life. That was a closed book for me. I wanted very much to close that book, not the chapter but the whole book.

> You don't have much choice, you don't think, you don't have time to think about it. You just have to move on and that was nothing compared to what I have survived in Sarajevo that was easy in this country. You just go on, start thinking OK I'm in the new country, I want to see what is best thing for me to do now is and you do the best thing, the thing you think is best.

The theme describes how these women did not want to think about their past and just wanted to look forward. Summerfield (1996) points out that the accepted norm within western culture is that victims of traumatic events should work through what they had experienced and some professionals believe that personal recovery cannot be achieved without psychological help. These psychologists, Summerfield adds, assume that if victims seem to be coping well and managing their lives, the real problem is hidden; but what they do not recognize are the norms, traditions, and the coping mechanisms of refugees, which are based on their cultural beliefs. Furthermore, when the interviewed women were asked where they thought their home was, they all paused and looked rather moved by the question. It was difficult for them to respond and they took a long time to answer. Their answers were very short; the tone of their voice was different and they were feeling rather puzzled.

Home is where you feel good and I feel good here at the moment. I feel very satisfied with my life at the moment, so I think London is my home. Bosnia is lovely, lovely past.

Where is home now, I don't know. I don't know really. It is as confusing as it is, I don't know. If I go back home to Sarajevo I don't feel that is home, although I was born there; but when I come here to London, I don't feel this is home as well.

Home is wherever I pay rent. And I try to make it nice by trying to make it functionally useful, but there is no real home. It is just where I make it; having a place here is not as it was back home in Bosnia.

There appeared to be some discomfort raised by this question. Understandably, it is difficult for displaced refugees to know where home is. They all stated in one way or the other that home was in the UK. Although they kept saying they felt settled in the UK and did not want to go back to Bosnia, they all called their native country "back home". They did not want to return to Bosnia, but could not leave it behind completely.

Reflection

The interviewed refugee women in this study were asked to tell their stories, to share their personal experiences of being refugees. The themes which emerged from their stories were analysed from a phenomenological perspective, seeing their difficulties, struggles, and their emotions as part of their being in the world. The study employed the existential attitude of seeing these refugees as active interpreters of their past and present experiences and how they created the meaning of their world (van Deurzen-Smith, 1998). The study was about giving these women refugees the opportunity to speak for themselves and describe their lives from their own subjective perspectives. They shared their stories about their struggles and recalled some painful memories. They expressed a view of having wanted to be seen as individuals who deserved support and assistance in ways that they felt were appropriate.

Therefore, this study was primarily focused on listening to them and their experiences. The aim was to try to understand their perspective of their needs and how their accounts could be used to help professionals gain an understanding of clients' perspectives.

The consequences of war may or may not lead to changes in mental health, and professionals should not make any assumptions. As is evident in this study, reactions to such difficult events in life depended greatly upon the individual interpretations of their circumstances. Frankl (1962) stated that the meaning, the constant search for the understanding of life events, is central to the motivation of the individuals.

These women were able to integrate their refugee experiences in a positive way. They recognized what they could gain from living in exile and, therefore, saw it as an opportunity to rebuild their lives. One of the main features of this study is the understanding that they needed support and assistance, which they described as useful at the time. Professional help, such as counselling, initially was seen in accordance with the traditional medical view they held in their native country. Their view was that they were not "crazy" and, therefore, did not seek such help. However, after a few years of living in their new country they became familiar with the notion of counselling. They were willing to accept new views and talked openly about their preconception of counselling. Perhaps when they had been offered counselling, they could not understand what counselling meant. They were not aware of counselling services as they exist in the UK, and did not value such services as helpful. Furthermore, these refugee women believed that their lives were not normal, and perhaps the struggle to change this helped them pick up the pieces of their shattered lives and rebuild what they thought would be a normal life. They may not have seen things as they were, but they saw them as they experienced them.

This study cannot be assumed to represent the entire Bosnian refugee population. It was about these four refugees and their stories. Moreover, the refugee sample selection may be skewed by the preference for refugees who spoke English. This may represent participants who were more able to integrate into the new society. The study did not take into consideration gender differences, life history, or social class. This was because the interviewed refugees agreed to participate on the basis of disclosing as many or as few personal details as they wished. The anonymity may have given them the courage to tell their stories freely. Therefore, the inter-viewed women were seen as part of their culture, which was completely damaged and disintegrated owing to the war. They come from a community that during the war became ethnically divided; the masses grouped themselves according to their religion, and these women may have felt ashamed to talk about it. They may have felt ashamed to be identified with the war in their country. They wanted to put the past behind them and have a new life. Living in exile, they had the opportunity to do this.

When they agreed to participate in the study, they did not feel sufficiently at ease to tell me their life stories prior to reaching the UK. Perhaps, their attitude was to see me as intruding into their privacy. Maybe it reminded them of having been asked questions in the past which they did not like. It may have reminded them of the Home Office type questions regarding their immigration status. Even though they had been living in this country for some years, they were still wary about talking to a stranger about their refugee days. As long as they were in control, as long as they were decid-ing what to say, they felt safe. It seemed as if they wanted to tell their stories, but did not want potential readers to know who they were. This may have been a reason why one of them did not give permission for her story to be published—as if she could have been identified. They were private about themselves. Therefore, cultural characteristics are significant in determining how refugees respond to such events in their lives. Women in Bosnia are said to be able to cope with life difficulties, especially knowing they were living in a male-dominated society. Culturally, they have been brought up to be strong, confident, and able to manage changes in their lives. Perhaps this attitude guided them through their difficulties in living in exile. One of the points for further research could be to compare Bosnian men and women, and their similarities and differences in coping with dramatic life changes.

Furthermore, these women often felt misunderstood by people they came across. They had preconceptions of counselling and they felt that people in the new country could not understand their needs. Thus, they searched for their own ways of coping. These women refugees seemed to have the capacity to manage change in their lives. They seemed confident and managed the transition from one culture to another. They were able to hold on to their beliefs and hopes and to use their friends and family as support in order to overcome their difficulties. This is an important feature of this study, in that it emphasizes that working with refugees involves listening to their needs and encouraging their capacity to rebuild their lives. Any misunderstanding of refugees and their needs could be avoided if refugees are asked to explain how they perceive their situation and what meaning they address to it, instead of seeing them from the western theories, where the focus is on the individual and the larger social context is overlooked. Alayarian (2007), in describing the work of the Refugee Therapy Centre in London, writes about the importance of listening to refugees.

What is not so evident in the text presented, but what I heard these women describe, is that they felt they were not alone in their experiences. They formed a network of friends who could help, support, and encourage them. This was the way they dealt with difficulties in their native country, by discussing the issues with friends and family members. For them, their experiences of exile and the memories of the war were not to be discussed with a psychologist, whom they thought would not understand them anyway. It is, therefore, obvious how social factors played an important role for these refugees in the process of coping with their life changes. One could say their therapeutic experience was to be accepted by the host country as equal citizens, where they felt valued and respected. Harris (2007) points out the importance of social support.

Overall, the personal stories of these women refugees analysed in this study are consistent with findings of Richters (1998), who wrote about how western professionals came to Sarajevo with already established notions of the nature of the problems, knowing very little or nothing about the culture, political and social situations, but with in-depth knowledge of post traumatic stress disorder, as had been written in their textbooks. Professionals had no time to think about their interventions, to reflect upon the appropriateness of their help, and were unaware of the traditional ways of coping with stress as seen in Bosnia. Similar findings were described by Giller (1998) while establishing a trauma project in Uganda with her colleagues. They were there to provide psychological help and the local people were more concerned about finding money, jobs, and schools. It became obvious to them that the help they were providing was not what the local people wanted. They could not fully understand how people coped without any psychotherapeutic help, but were aware that the local people were resilient to incredible conditions of the war and they coped. During their stay in Uganda they observed,

> In whatever ways they managed to do it, Ugandans were coping with the results of some of the worst calamities imaginable, and the last thing they needed was a centre that could only serve to show them that their ways of coping were ultimately inferior. [Giller, 1998, p. 13]

Furthermore, Tribe and De Silva (1999) described their work with war widows in a refugee camp in Sri Lanka. Their aim was to promote mental health among the refugees, mainly by facilitating their coping strategies. They emphasized the need for empowering these women, rather than treating them. Their aim was to give information, provide skills and training, helping women to use and maximize their own potentials.

This study represents these four women refugees and their life stories and, therefore, cannot be generalized. They speak only for themselves. They showed how experiences of being refugees could be both overwhelming and strengthening. They gave their experiences personal meanings and found their own ways of dealing with their difficulties. It is my hope that their voices will be heard not only by professionals working with refugees, but by many others.

References

Alayarian, A. (Ed.) (2007). *Resilience, Suffering, and Creativity: The Work of the Refugee Therapy Centre*. London: Karnac.

Berry, J. (1997). Immigration, acculturation and adaptation. *Applied Psychology: An International Review, 46*(1): 5–34.

Blackwell, D. (2005). *Counselling and Psychotherapy for Refugees.* London: Jessica Kingsley.

Bracken, P., Giller, J., & Summerfield, D. (1997). Rethinking mental health work with survivors of wartime violence and refugees. *Journal of Refugee Studies, 10*(4): 431–442.

Ehrenberg, D. B. (2007). How I became a psychoanalyst. In: A. Alayarian (Ed.), *Resilience, Suffering, and Creativity. The Work of the Refugee Therapy Centre* (pp. 111–139). London: Karnac.

Frankl, V. E. (1962). *Man's Search for Meaning.* London: Hodder and Stoughton.

Harris, T. (2007). Loss of network support piled on trauma: thinking more broadly about the context of refugees. In: A. Alayarian (Ed.). *Resilience, Suffering, and Creativity. The Work of the Refugee Therapy Centre* (pp. 81–96). London: Karnac.

Giller, J. (1998). Caring for "victims of torture" in Uganda: some personal reflections. In: P. Bracken & C. Petty (Eds.), *Rethinking the Trauma of War* (pp. 128–145). London: Free Association Books.

Loizos, P. (2002). Misconceiving refugees? In: R. K. Papadopoulos (Ed.), *Therapeutic Care for Refugees. No Place Like Home* (pp. 41–56). London: Karnac.

Papadopoulos, R. K. (Ed.) (2002). *Therapeutic Care for Refugee. No Place Like Home.* London: Karnac.

Richman, R. (1998). Looking before and after: refugees and asylum seekers in the West. In: P. Bracken & C. Petty (Eds.), *Rethinking the Trauma of War* (pp. 170–186). London: Free Association Books.

Richters, A. (1998). Sexual violence in wartime. Psycho-sociocultural wounds and healing processes: the example of the former Yugoslavia. In: P. Bracken & C. Petty (Eds.). *Rethinking the Trauma of War* (pp. 112–127). London: Free Association Books.

Summerfield, D. (1995). Raising the dead: war, reparation and the politics of memory. *British Medical Journal, 311*: 495–497.

Summerfield, D. (1996). *The Impact of War and Atrocity on Civilian Populations: Basic Principles for NGO Interventions and a Critique of Psychological Trauma Projects.* Relief and Rehabilitation Network Paper 14. London: Overseas Development Institute.

Summerfield, D. (1999). A critique of seven assumptions behind psychological trauma programmes in war-affected areas. *Social Science and Medicine, 48*: 1449–1462.

Thomas, L. K. (2007). The therapeutic needs of those fleeing persecution and violence, now and in the future. In: A. Alayarian (Ed.), *Resilience, Suffering, and Creativity. The Work of the Refugee Therapy Centre* (pp. 45–61). London: Karnac.

Tribe, R., & de Silva, P. (1999). Psychological intervention with displaced widows in Sri Lanka. *International Review of Psychiatry, 11*: 184–190.

Van der Veer, G. (1998). *Counselling and Therapy with Refugees. Psychological Problems of Victims of War, Torture and Repression* (2nd edn). Chichester: Wiley.

Van Deurzen-Smith, E. (1998). *Existential Counselling in Practice.* London: Sage.

Psychotherapeutic work with refugees: understanding the therapist's countertransference

Zack Eleftheriadou

Most therapists are chosen to work with refugees because they speak the language or come from the same cultural or racial background and/or have had experiences that resonate with those of the client. They are often people who can easily understand the clients' experiences, which creates interesting and potent therapeutic dynamics. They can offer a great deal of support to the person, but often with the high risk of over-identification. This chapter is an attempt to examine the complex dynamics from the therapist's perspective when working with refugee clients. (The word "therapist" is used to refer to the professional working with refugees, using a psychodynamic therapeutic framework.) It is a collection of thoughts and feelings expressed in psychotherapeutic and supervisory work from different types of refugee mental health workers. It is an attempt to understand further the therapeutic relationship by focusing on the therapist's psychological response to the client. The chapter will outline briefly some of the common themes reported by refugees, but the primary aim is to focus on the therapist's *countertransference* feelings. Countertransference, in this context, is defined as a personal psychological response, as well as consisting of socio-political components.

The refugee experience

This chapter begins with a brief outline of the social experience often reported by refugee clients. The social experience and the internal individual experience are closely connected, but one cannot become a predictor of the other; that is, knowing about one's social experience does not imply that we know about their internal world (i.e., family life dynamics) and vice versa (i.e., that because we know a person's family dynamics we can predict exactly how they will behave in other social groups). Indeed, there is also a vast difference between one social context and another, so this is not an attempt to find commonalities between *all* refugee groups. Additionally, there is no doubt that people have different levels of resilience and coping skills (van der Veer, 1998).

Those that go through the experience of separation from their homeland have uniquely powerful and lasting experiences. As Herman so poignantly writes,

> Having come to terms with the traumatic past, the survivor faces the task of creating a future. She has mourned the old self that the trauma destroyed; now she must develop a new self. Her relationships have been tested and forever changed by the trauma; now she must develop new relationships. The old beliefs that gave meaning to her life have been challenged; now she must find anew a sustaining faith . . . In accomplishing this work, the survivor reclaims her world. [1992, p. 196]

It has often been thought that that refugees "need" counselling or psychotherapy, but the reality is that many people need other resources, such as housing, etc, when they first enter a new country. Also, there may not be access to counselling immediately, mainly due to urgent practical factors, such as financial or housing constraints. This may mean that the abrupt nature of events and the shock of the experience frequently cannot be processed until a later stage. Some theorists have compared the refugee experience to post traumatic stress disorder (PTSD), where flashbacks of the experience return much later, often years after the original event (Caruth, 1995). It is not uncommon to hear clients recall experiences and dreams for the first time some years after the actual experience. This chapter will not go through the rather complex and controversial arguments of whether the refugee experience is indeed PTSD or is of a different nature. Instead, the author recognizes that, for many, *being denied the rite of farewell can be both a damaging and a lasting experience*. It touches on other early experiences and fears of abandonment, which to the refugee become a reality. The "weaning process" with the mother country has not had a chance to take place and there may be a strong attachment to it for a long time; to some extent this never ceases, as one's birthplace always remains "special". This is like a developmental process, where the person needs to leave his own familiar framework and "mirroring" (Winnicott, 1971) structures and find something in the new environment. Facing up to the impossibility of return and letting go of the hope of seeing people and places again may be the most difficult to relinquish. Fantasies may fill in for not having any news, that those left behind may be "dead", in reality or in mind. There is forever the wish to meet again, and it is so connected to the fear that we shall never meet again. It is vital that loss and mourning are allowed to take place, or what has been called *cultural bereavement* (Eisenbruch, 1984); this literally means the loss of the mother country.

Being forced to evacuate one's country brings about fury at not being able to plan and know when you will leave, endless wondering on how safe one will be, and whether there is going to be a return or not. The experience of anger, resentment, bitterness, and frustration at having had to flee something is unlike the experience of immigrants who have left a country out of choice, and have arrived motivated to look for something, usually idealized, in the new culture. It is important to establish to what extent the person feels able to reconstruct or recreate part of his/her environment in the new country. Undoubtedly, how much the new country is facilitating this process, psychologically, physically, and economically, will also have an impact.

It is a common wish to treat survivors as heroes when they arrive in the new country. They may feel enormous relief about being free, but for the survivors the feeling of guilt is carried for those that were left behind; the anxiety about what has happened to them, whether they have survived, and the fear of what it would have been like to have remained in the homeland under occupation (Grinberg & Grinberg, 1989).

Children who have been adopted do not usually display problems until they are adopted. They have to make the new parents suffer because, paradoxically, they now feel safer than they felt in the past. In the same way, for refugees, the relationship to the new country can sometimes be seen as the cause of their problems rather than the country they fled from. However, sometimes it is easier for them to see it in this light than to have angry feelings for their own country. For some, there may be a feeling that they are imprisoned because they have had to leave and that they cannot go back. As Grinberg and Grinberg state, "they [refugees] did not travel toward something but were fleeing or expelled from something, and they are bitter, resentful, frustrated" (1989, p. 158).

The first few sessions will bring out many of the client's forthcoming themes and provide some idea where the area of conflicts and trauma might be. The person's story will unfold in its own time. Cultural reminiscing is so much part of the refugee experience, and counselling/psychotherapy might be the first and, perhaps, for some, the only safe space to think about the ties with the past. There may be nostalgia, which is an important link to the past, but it has its flip side, where a person can get completely engrossed in the past so that it becomes impossible to have or want a relationship with the present or even the future. Zwingmann (1982) named this as the "nostalgic paradox", referring to the positive and the negative; referring to what one wants from the past and what one does not wish to have from the present. Working with this is often the delicate balance of the therapeutic work, revisiting and remembering and, at the same time, encouraging a live relationship with the present and being able to think about a future.

The psychological response of the therapist

Countertransference is a complicated process, and it consists of not only what is evoked by the client's material, but how it makes an individual therapist react, linked to their personal history. However, for the purposes of this chapter, I have outlined some of the most common countertransference reactions evoked by this client group.

Countertransference has become one of the most commonly discussed and valued therapeutic skills. Winnicott talked about the delicate role of the therapist: "the psychotherapist must remain vulnerable, and yet retain his professional role in his actual working hours" (1988, p. 264). He goes on to say, "the analyst will need to remain orientated to external reality while in fact being identified with the patient, even merged with the patient" (*ibid.*, p. 267). This may sound like a contradiction, but it really describes how complex and skilled a therapist has to be in order to analyse the other.

On the one hand, the therapist has to feel what the client is feeling, but there has to be enough distance that the therapist can digest the experience and wonder about it with the client. This space is desirable for the two parties, the client and therapist, to function as two rather than to merge into one. It is also a space where the therapist can create distance from his or her own countertransference feelings. As Racker suggests, countertransference is both the most dangerous occurrence in psychotherapy and the most useful tool. It helps to know "what should be interpreted and when" (Racker, 1988, p. 160). It is now considered to be a two-way process between the client and the therapist. Countertransference is the therapist's response to the client's "real and imaginary transferences" (p. 161) and the transference is "the response to the analyst's imaginary and real countertransferences" (*ibid.*, pp. 161–162). Furthermore, the therapist's response consists of the "present and past, the continuous and intimate connection of reality and fantasy, of external and internal, conscious and unconscious" (*ibid.*, p. 163). This is crucial to keep in mind so that we do not make the client's experience too similar to ours. If we follow this path (i.e., over-identify with the client) because it triggers so much of our own experience, it will, in turn, be reflected in our interpretations that we can no longer see any differences with our client (van der Veer, 1998).

In his context, countertransference is the response of the therapist, but it is important to emphasize that it is not free of the socio-political context and beliefs of the therapist. A cross-cultural therapist does not need to know everything about their clients' socio-political backgrounds, but it is *necessary to have some information about the other's context and how it might be different from the therapist's*. Many workers who work with refugees also suggest that the therapist needs to have thought carefully about their political stance and ideas about human rights (Sodowsky, Kuo-Jackson, & Loya, 1997). Many clients will not only pick up the therapist's stance, but will challenge it and demand that it is made explicit. It is necessary in such work to demonstrate "a general human rights commitment" (Turner, 1992, p. 167). Of course, this does not in any way guarantee a strong therapeutic alliance, since it is likely that the therapist adheres strongly to one political ideology. Inevitably, working with clients who believe in different political regimes will stir up strong feelings.

The therapist can feel bombarded by the trauma just as much as the client. The therapist may defend by denial of the events they are hearing, may feel deskilled and discouraged, or experience complete despair and astonishment at the level of human destructiveness (Turner, 1992). Therapists may find themselves asking more questions, those that they would normally not need to ask, and usually only do so for the purposes of clarification. It may result that the trauma is not talked about and the therapist addresses everything, but the trauma. Suddenly, there may be the realization that the therapist does not know anything of the client's life events. These unconscious messages are picked up by the client and can be either a way of not examining their own feelings or being stopped from doing so because, be it on an unconscious level, they sense they have overwhelmed the therapist. It can be experienced as if one has flooded the therapist and s/he cannot hear any more.

One of the common countertransference feelings is to treat the person as if they have had no life existence before coming to the host country. This can be seen commonly in referral letters that give no information about the person prior to the move to the new country. Psychotherapy, of course, needs to focus on the person as a whole. We need to have a continuity of the person and information about their lives before they became refugees. Past, present, and future are all there, intertwined, and need to be explored sensitively. Being a refugee is part of the experience, but there are also many other components. Also, this may be how the client portrays themselves in their desperate attempts to "fit in", to "forget", or to deal with the disappointment with their own country for not (safely) "holding" and "containing" them. Furthermore, not only is the whole external experience traumatic, but it can evoke further past and new internal and family conflicts. Sometimes, these are intensified in the new country, because the family is no longer buffered by the extended family system or other community systems, such as social and religious groups.

There may be another occurrence where the therapist is so overwhelmed by the material that they cut off from the emotional content; instead, they become rather impulsive in seeking information. This may take the form of constantly asking questions about the events and, unnecessarily, structuring the session. The healing for the client will take place with the help of building the "secure base" (Bowlby, 1979); initially, that base may be the therapeutic space. If the relationship is stable and boundaries are kept, then the client will feel they are in a safe environment.

Herman discusses the impact of this on the therapist, stating that

the patient's symptoms simultaneously call attention to the existence of an unspeakable secret and deflect attention from that secret ... Therapists often report uncanny, grotesque or bizarre imagery dreams, fantasies while working with such patients. They may themselves have unaccustomed dissociative experiences, including not only numbing and perceptual distortions but also depersonalization, derealization, and passive influence experiences. [1992, p. 146]

Case example: Mona

Mona, who was in her late thirties, had left Beirut twenty years prior to seeking psychotherapy. She had been residing in the UK for a few years. When I asked her about her background, one of the first things she said was that their house was destroyed by the bombing during the war. In terms of her profession, she was an interpreter who had worked on news programmes in different countries. When I asked her about her command of so many different languages, she explained that she had learnt languages at school. She had added that it had, therefore, made sense for her to go into interpreting as a career. I would often feel as if I was part of a simultaneous translation programme during our sessions. She would say something and then say it in another language. At first I thought it was important that she was bringing all the languages to the therapy, but then I sensed there was immense anxiety attached, which would be dealt with by translating and therefore interpreting. I began to be intrigued about how she used language in the therapeutic setting and wondered what role it had in preserving feelings she had had for some years. She was curious about my own background (although she knew where I came from) and she said, "That is one language I don't speak!" and smiled. She seemed so relieved when she said this, and I wondered if she was saying to me that there was one adult language she did not speak and did not therefore have to take responsibility. I put this to her and she looked at me curiously, responding that she still thought that Greek was a nice language, and if she had the chance she would like to learn it. It was striking, though, that in subsequent sessions the sense of having to (rather tirelessly) translate and distance herself from emotion had decreased significantly.

In subsequent sessions, we spoke more about the many times her family had to flee from their home. I said it sounded as if she had become the main communicator for her family. She said it was not something she had really thought about in those terms. As she recalled more of the events around the build-up of the bombing and the fleeing, she said she had felt she had helped her family. Soon after, she spoke of the guilt of having broken the family hierarchy by becoming involved in areas she would have not normally been part of as a child and also as a girl. Her younger brother was also multi-lingual, but had been too young at the time of the evacuation to be of assistance with formal documents, etc. In later years, her job had also taken her to areas where there was political unrest and often she would find herself in unsafe places. She said she never had allowed herself to feel the pain. The therapeutic exploration continued for some years.

Mastery of a life event such as Mona's is largely dependent on one's psychological state, the conscious and unconscious influence and models one sees around them. Although it is important that the therapist is able to find ways that they can support the client and feel there can be some control, therapists often report feeling less efficient, forgetting about things they would normally remember, and generally having less professional control. Mona was an extremely intelligent woman who had used her language skills to her best ability. It was a strength which she had used and, indeed, continued using, but it was also time to recognize all the feelings which had been so deeply buried that they were creating a great deal of conflict.

The question of language is of great importance when the therapist and client come from different backgrounds. If the client and therapist can only communicate with the therapist's language, it should be explored, preferably early on in the therapy. For some people, it may give protection from chaos, and for others it intensifies it. In Mona's case, language had become protective and a way of fitting in to new environments. There is no doubt that learning a language can contribute greatly to being part of a new culture, but it is not an automatic, emotional passport into the culture. Mona had tired herself out by always being alert and listening out, trying to feel in control by understanding everything around her. These issues were, of course, connected to many other themes in her life, including the many separations she had had from her family, especially her mother, around the time of the war, which made her become extremely alert. During the separations it was a way of comforting herself that her parents would come back to "rescue" her.

Countertransference of the therapist can include feelings of hopelessness and helplessness, a sense of paralysis and impotence. It becomes necessary not to create secondary victimization; that is, to inflict further aggression, especially to those who have been tortured. Powerlessness of the therapist can easily be turned into antipathy for the client (who cannot be helped and is evoking too many strong feelings), or, for many psychiatrists, it may result in unnecessary medication in order to be of help and, hence, remain the powerful professional.

In hearing the stories, therapists can often feel a sense of fragmentation, and it is important to restore a sense of dignity and respect for the person. The task of turning the perverse experience of torture and being able to experience a healing relationship is a long and difficult one. The therapist may struggle to encourage the person to reclaim a sense of space, self, body, and mind as they hear from the client of how they have been abused by the persecutor. Similarly, the therapist can experience a fear that, like the client who feels they will never be rid of the oppressor, they cannot get rid of the client's stories. It becomes vital to tune in to the client's individual level of tolerance of such experiences and, subsequently, the ability to re-experience them in therapy. Ambiguous feelings towards the torturer may have to be explored, which may also be unconsciously transferred to the therapist. This may be evoked further in some cases where the aggressor is of a similar ethnic background to that of the therapist. It is then the responsibility of the therapist to address it with the client early on in the therapy and be aware of its intensity as the therapy progresses.

Furthermore, there can be a strong suspicion of the therapist. After all, many have been through experiences where they completely lost faith in other human beings. The therapist may have a strong wish to compensate for the client by "giving" too much, such as not finishing on time or, when appropriate, not challenging enough.

If the therapist and the client have been through similar experiences and / or share a culture or language, an unconscious competition can also be evoked between them as to who has been through worse atrocities than the other. Another common theme is that the client can try to paint a rosy picture in order not to make the therapist suffer in the way they did (especially if they know they share a socio-political background). If they have not been able to bear the experience, it may be difficult to believe that their therapist, who comes from the same background, has also suffered. They are trying to protect themselves from what they have experienced by splitting off the trauma feelings from other experiences or memories. This takes place between themselves and the therapist, by attributing the experience or projecting it into the therapist, but, of course, ultimately it is trying to expel it from their own psyche. It is common to tell the therapist details that do not have any emotional affect attached to them.

Supervision and support

Support for the therapist is vital in this type of work. The work can progress only if the therapist is able to make sense of his or her own emotional reactions to clients. However experienced they are, they will need to parallel the client's process on a regular basis. By "parallel", I mean that their emotional reactions to the client's story will need to be monitored at each stage of the therapy. Questions such as why did a specific part of the story make the therapist feel sad, or if there was another part of the story they could not relate to, and even found themselves drifting into what appeared to be an unrelated theme, then they need to understand what the client is communicating and how they are reacting. Of course, at all times, the therapist's reaction will be a result of an interaction of their own psychology, family, and culture.

Of course, the supervisor also needs to be skilled and have experience in working with refugees. Often the client–therapist dynamic, especially when feelings are still raw, becomes re-enacted between the supervisor and the therapist. This parallel process between the different parties, or the supervisor's and therapist's countertransferences, need to be worked through carefully. For example, if the therapist working with the refugee client takes the therapeutic material to supervision, it may take time to work out with the supervisor when the therapist (unconsciously) takes on the client's issues and the supervisor carries the therapist's material. There are many different scenarios that can take place, depending on what kind of identifications are formed; that is, which aspects the therapist takes on board or resonates with, and which ones the supervisor is in touch with. This demonstrates that countertransference can be equally powerful within the supervisory relationship and can evoke many of the counselling themes mentioned earlier, and it is, therefore, essential that it is addressed.

In conclusion, this chapter is important because it outlines the part of the transcultural therapeutic work with refugees/survivors of torture that may remain unexplored because it raises too many painful emotions for us, as therapists. This does not mean that other clients do not raise similar countertransference themes (including strong defences) in us, but refugee clients have had unique social experiences that have a powerful impact on their individual ways of functioning. In the same way, the therapists I spoke to and supervised who work with refugees, as well as my own personal and professional experiences with refugee clients, have common defences which are triggered during these therapeutic encounters. These common themes will be experienced from our own psychic reference point. Therapeutic work with refugee clients is extremely rewarding, but painful, especially to those who have been through similar experiences. Understanding our part in the relationship can free the client to begin to explore and understand their emotional world. Since the client and therapist can often mirror each other's feelings, without unravelling the therapist's countertransference reactions we cannot fully support and understand the client's (unconscious) experience. *Hence, personal development and supervision in this type of work is not only desirable and useful, but of absolute necessity.* It is a way of constantly monitoring and ensuring that we do not get too involved in the client's emotional experience and, paradoxically, it often means that we gain more insight into our client's stories through our own emotional reactions to them.

References

Bowlby, J. (1979). *The Making and Breaking of Affectational Bonds*. London: Routledge.

Caruth, C. (Ed) (1995). *Trauma: Explorations in Memory*. Baltimore, MD: Johns Hopkins University Press.

Eisenbruch, M. (1984). Cross-cultural aspects of bereavement II: ethnic and cultural variations in the development of bereavement practices. *Culture, Medicine and Psychiatry*, 8(4): 315–347.

Grinberg, L., & Grinberg, R. (Eds.) (1989). *Psychoanalytic Perspectives on Migration and Exile*. New Haven, CT: Yale University Press.

Herman, J. (1992). *Trauma and Recovery*. New York: Basic Books.

Racker, H. (1988). *Transference and Countertransference*. London: Karnac.

Sodowsky, G. R., Kuo-Jackson, P. Y., & Loya, G. L. (1997). Outcome of training in the philosophy of assessment, multicultural counselling competencies. In: D. B. Popo-Davis & H. L. K. Coleman (Eds.), *Multicultural Counselling Competencies* (pp. 3–42). Thousand Oaks, CA: Sage.

Turner, S. W. (1992). Therapeutic approaches with survivors of torture. In: J. Kareem & R. Littlewood (Eds.), *Intercultural Therapy* (pp. 163–174). London: Blackwell Scientific.

Van der Veer, G. (1998). *Counselling and Therapy with Refugees and Victims of Trauma*, Chichester: Wiley.

Winnicott, D. W. (1971). *Playing and Reality*, London: Routledge.

Winnicott, D. W. (1988). Counter-transference. In: B. Wolstein (Ed.), *Essential Papers on Countertransference* (pp. 262–269). New York: New York University Press.

Zwingmann, C. (1982). *"Heimweh" or "Nostalgic Reaction": A Conceptual Analysis and Interpretation of Medico–Psychological Phenomenon.* Stanford, CA: Stanford University Press.

CHAPTER ELEVEN

Psychodynamic considerations for diversity consultancy in organizations

Aileen Alleyne

This chapter discusses psychodynamic considerations for diversity consultancy in organizations where the challenge to address wide-ranging issues of difference is paramount.

To put this topic into context, we must first acknowledge that the workplace can be a major source of daily stress, conflict, and disruptive change. Harm to personal well-being and poor organizational relationships can be the result, and these factors can threaten workplace efficiency as well as the organization's reputation. Added to this, when tensions and misunderstandings from cultural and racial differences exist, workplace difficulties can often be exacerbated, leading to gridlock and breakdown. External consultancy can be an important intervention to enable organizations to work with these conflicts and develop ways of reducing conflict and boosting workplace morale and productivity.

Organizational consultancy can provide a range of services that could incorporate training, supervision, independent and impartial advice, direction, group facilitation, and mediation. The consultant's role is to work collaboratively with employers and their employees to help them examine both their individual and organizational work practices, set realistic goals, develop ways to work effectively with diversity, and create an atmosphere of equality and inclusion for all. External consultancy can also be seen as an investment, which may work out as being cost-productive to organizations that may otherwise become trapped and embroiled in expensive complaints procedures. Consultancy, in this respect, can help repair damage brought about by old workplace cultures that have gone unchallenged over time. Experienced consultants will be able to offer a combination of psychotherapeutic, organizational, groupwork, coaching and teaching skills, as well as provide impartial and expert support designed for damage limitation and developing reflexive practices for achieving effective organizational outcomes.

In the first instance, this chapter will offer a critique of diversity consultancy and then go on to discuss some unheeded dimensions of working in this area. The author will argue that effective diversity consultancy in organizations must include attention to both "micro" (subtle and unconscious) and "macro" (external and conscious) processes in order to meet the challenge and task of understanding complex issues of difference and diversity. The author will focus mainly on "micro" processes, since relatively little attention is given to this important area. To elaborate, psychodynamic considerations will be discussed from the perspective of planning and executing organizational consultancy contracts. Specific conceptual themes related to black–white dynamics operating in workplace contexts will be highlighted, as well as discussion about the pitfalls and rewards of working with different level group challenges in this area. The chapter's overall message supports the role of diversity consultancy as a good investment for organizations in meeting ever-present and ever-changing challenges in managing workplace diversity issues today.

London, as a focus for this chapter's topic, is well known for its international identity, richness of cultures, and openness to embracing diverse racial groups from the world over. Yet, in the provision of adequate services to minorities and visible representation of Black, Asian, and Minority Ethnic (BAME) individuals at all levels of employment, there is a very different picture. Service providers remain complicit in their attitudes towards engaging fully in diversity initiatives and a culture of complacency continues to be an issue to be challenged.

In contrast to the 1980s and early 1990s, when "Racism Aware-ness Training" (RAT) was mandatory and generally problematic in organizations, current needs for training and consultancy appear to be better recognized and less openly resisted. However, what we now address as "diversity consultancy" is still met with many diffi-culties. As a facilitator and consultant contributing to this area for the past eighteen years, I am able to draw on wide-ranging experi-ences and acquired knowledge to be able to offer a constructive critique and alternatives for working more effectively in this area.

In the past, popular approaches to diversity consultancy tended to focus largely on "macro" processes. This perspective addressed the more obvious inequities and power dynamics within the social, environmental, economic, and political structures of our society. The focus of this type of consultancy provided a system of review for organizations to examine their structures, which included the workforce makeup, employment practices, management policies, and service delivery in an ever-changing population. The resulting appraisal sessions assisted organizations in their goals towards participating in diversity endeavours. However helpful this work was, my contention is that this "macro" approach was one-dimen-sional and, as a result, suffered many shortcomings. Consultancy was generally facilitated from a position of authority and offered highly prescriptive methods for implementation and change. These changes inadvertently had the effect of generating anger and resentment, as well as inducing shame, blame, crippling guilt, and compensatory attitudes in those taking part. Unsurprisingly, "macro" consultancy was met with resistance and often ran the risk of intimidating the already cautious and cynical participant and employer. Outcomes proved poor, and many organizations remained entrenched in old and negative attitudes. An impasse contributed to a climate of political correctness, and a lip-service approach towards the real objectives of embracing diversity became the order of the day. Many painful and expensive lessons were learnt during this difficult period spanning the 1980s and 1990s. The resulting scars left an atmosphere of cynicism and doubt about the importance of embracing diversity initiatives.

A decade of unsatisfactory learning outcomes highlighted a need for effective diversity consultancy to include close attention to both "micro" and "macro" processes. As previously mentioned, "micro" processes focus on the more subtle and challenging aspects of personal and interpersonal dynamics in human relationship. Perhaps one of the trickiest is dealing with challenges inherent in working with black–white racism. "Micro" processes can enable closer scrutiny of subtle dynamics underpinning unconscious behaviours towards differences in this and all other kinds of differences.

"Micro" processes facilitate exploration of different styles of thinking, communicating, and relating, as well as deepening understanding of how cultural and social history have an impact on cultural beliefs and value systems and, in turn, shape identity and being in the world. A psychodynamic approach to thinking about these areas can deepen exploration of the multitude of reactions towards difference, such as managing natural feelings of discomfort, anxiety, and not knowing, as well as reframing negative and harmful reactions of bigotry and hate. Deeper awareness of these areas can increase confidence in working with the unknown and unfamiliar as well as strengthen individual competence and organizational power to effect lasting change in diversity pursuits.

Although the main aim of "micro" processes in organizational diversity consultancy is to address issues of difference, there is also an underlying therapeutic endeavour to include and embrace areas of commonality and sameness that unite diverse groups and cultures. This is most important in preventing splits and the pathologizing of what is different.

The challenge for the consultant employing the "micro" approach is to be more facilitative and less didactic. The aim is to bring together teaching methods that enable critical analysis of human behaviour, while encouraging direct personal learning from the group membership and a development of cultural reflexivity in participants. Cultural reflexivity is used in this context to address personal challenges necessary in dealing with unconscious identifications and fixations with aspects of one's history that lead to complexes and the narrowing of our horizons. Although the "micro" approach can prove more personally challenging for the facilitator and uncomfortable for group participants, effective facilitation can be achieved through respecting the intent of the work, which is not to induce guilt, shame, oppress the other, or create divisiveness among members. The "micro" approach is far removed from the kind of consultancy that was once perceived as training for "political correctness".

Executing diversity consultancy using the "micro" approach can be achieved through an array of exercises that guide participants to look initially at themselves as cultural beings before going on to explore differences in other racial and cultural groups. These activities can be facilitated in couples, triads, small groups, and large groups. Timely tutorial inputs can address themes such as power and powerlessness, cultural shame, internalized oppression, identity formation, and so on, in order to deepen participants' knowledge of the relevant cross-cultural concepts. Close examination of particular cross-cultural relationships can foster deeper understanding of those dynamics that are more subtle and difficult to pin down. Examples can be found in the complicated workings of institutional racism and its damaging effects. The consultant can include visual aids material relevant to these topics to diversify teaching methods and foster deeper clarity. Clear and realistic plans of action should be set with the organization to assess what can be realistically achieved, and follow-up trainings should be encouraged to evaluate and monitor the organization's initial objectives for bringing about change. Consultants can help employers with the knowledge that diversity consultancy is not an isolated or one-off event, but, rather, a rolling programme of training to achieve and maintain success. Consultants should be frank about the implications of organizations offering lip-service to diversity consultancy and suggest helpful guidelines for a more committed and purposeful approach to the aims and intentions of diversity management.

Understanding dynamics at the request stage

Pre-transference issues

It would be true to say that all that takes place before a consultancy contract begins will influence the *pre-transference* working relationship. Pre-transference is a term used by Curry (1964) to describe a number of factors, such as views, opinions, and ideas that are held about someone or a group long before we have met them or have established a relationship with them. Pre-transference holds our prejudices and fears about the unknown and unfamiliar. This factor, therefore, pre-determines and distorts perception of what is real and contributes to the makings of negative and unfavourable constructs about difference. In organizational consultancy, significant factors can determine the pre-transference relationship. These may include examples such as the language used by an organization to describe their training needs, for example, "the team has requested some cross-cultural training", or "the organization would like to know why black women are not using our services". In the first example, the term "cross-cultural training" would appear as a *catch-all* term used conveniently or carelessly to include everything and anything that is different to the majority's *norm*. The consultant can safely assume that the organization has not prepared or thought through its training needs, and should seek to clarity the specifics about the work to be undertaken.

Similarly, the second request unwittingly implies blame of black women who are not using the organization's services. The agency's intentions would be reflected differently if reworded: "We would like to explore ways in which we can attract more black women to our services". Blame is not implied in this example, and the organization is seen in its intent to be proactive and inclusive. These subtle dynamics of language are only one aspect of pre-transference dynamics. They inform the consultant of the group's level of awareness and unconscious training needs.

Other factors influencing the pre-transference relationship are concerned with the amount of funds and time made available for diversity consultancy, alongside issues regarding the racial makeup and cultural mix of a group, which are also important determinants to the effectiveness of consultancy initiatives. Organizations allocating too little time to thinking through these concerns may unwittingly marginalize the importance of the subject. Conversely, over-investing in diversity consultancy by, for example, throwing unspent budgets at this training area, can create difficulties for the consultant who becomes drawn into these dynamics.

Assuming all the above pre-transference issues can be satisfactorily addressed, a consultant will be in a much better position to plan and shape the consultancy. Groups that comprise a white majority membership and a tokenistic black or Asian member are likely to encounter certain difficulties that arise within such a group makeup. A tokenistic member can easily be pushed into being spokesperson for his or her cultural/racial group and be made to feel burdened and pressured into teaching their peers about race and cultural matters. Inevitably, their own needs will be marginalized. The consultant should be alert to conscious and unconscious scapegoating or idealization of the minority member and be vigilant in guarding against these destructive dynamics in any such group setting. Training material should be carefully selected to allow balanced learning for both majority and minority members, as it is often the case that minority group needs are overshadowed.

The handling of other pre-transference factors is required, such as unnecessary delays that follow an initial request for diversity consultancy. This might suggest the organization's ambivalence and anxiety to follow through with the enquiry. Additionally, a consultant's reputation, good, bad, or indifferent, may precede her to influence the pre-relationship. In such instances, unrealistic expectations might be held and assumptions made about what can be realistically achieved in the consultancy. For all of these reasons, consultants need to feel prepared for the challenge of the work and elicit clear parameters for the consultancy request. Having knowledge of "why now?", what exactly the organization wants, what are the intended learning outcomes, how will outcomes will be used and measured, what is to be achieved by having the outcomes, how will change be monitored and maintained, are key questions for good preparation. Two examples of pre-questionnaires for shaping a contract of diversity consultancy are offered below.

Pre-questionnaire 1

Please complete the questionnaire below. All information will be treated in the strictest of confidence and used by the facilitator to create a realistic focus for the training.

(a) Please give your reasons why this day is happening *now*.
(b) Briefly indicate what you perceive as the main difficulties in the team.
(c) Describe the present leadership style of management.
(d) What is the *primary task* of your team? This is not a request for a list of duties, but a description of the *main or overall purpose* of the team's work.

(e)   What do *you* hold for your team? Are you aware of carrying anything unspoken for the rest of the team?
(f)   What do you want from the training? Please be realistic about what can be achieved in the allotted time.

Pre-questionnaire 2

1.   Have you previously participated in Equal Opportunity or Diversity training? If yes, please indicate how you found the training.
2.   What would you like this training to incorporate?
3.   What would you like to gain from the training?
4.   What relevance do you think the proposed training will have to the way you work and the overall service delivery?
5.   How will the training benefit the organization (a) staff (b) clients?
6.   Are there any specific ways you feel your organization can improve its service delivery to people from ethnic minority groups?
7.   Fewer people from ethnic minorities access your service. Do you have any ideas as to why this is the case?
8.   What client group/s do you have most dealings with and why?

To further demonstrate how powerful early dynamics can impact on the organizational consultancy, two brief situations are presented. The first example is the phenomenon I will term "blurring the focus" and the second example is a common occurrence I will refer to as "killing time".

Blurring the focus

Blurring the focus is a phenomenon highlighting the very confused way organizations can present their request for diversity consultancy. A typical such request may be phrased thus: "We would like to address Equal Opportunities Issues by finding out why black and Asian clients are not using our service". Surprisingly, this request may also include concerns about reviewing the organization's

Equal Opportunities policies and structures, and further still, a request to deal with needs of the team and the organization's wish to tackle difficult staff relationships in a racially mixed team. In this multi-layered request, it has been known for an organization to stretch this overloaded remit even further to encompass additional needs for managing transcultural issues in counselling and groupwork practice—all of which they would like to be done in one day of training!

Killing time

Killing time is a phenomenon that is indicative of unconscious dynamics at play in meeting difficulties of the organizational diversity challenge. These may be manifested in various ways. One such example is the creation of hierarchies which are formed by placing "other important organizational needs" in direct competition with diversity initiatives. Killing time can also be observed in the minimal amount of time given over to dealing with complex diversity training agendas, for example, allocating a few hours or half a day to the topic. Additionally, organizations can indulge unnecessarily in the polemics of jargon, buzz words, and definitions relating to Equal Opportunity and anti-discriminatory practices, all of which can be interpreted as resistance dynamics working unconsciously towards killing off allocated time. Inherent in these *defensive* activities is the minimizing of complex issues of difference and denying challenge to the self.

Analysis of the two aforementioned examples highlights several important issues. In the mishmash of the first example, referred to as "blurring the focus", the request is overloaded with a merging of needs and priorities. The organization's confusion is very apparent. The consultant can help the organization to separate out conflated needs and tasks and direct them to proceed in a more informed and structured manner in order to achieve realistic goals. A review of the tasks may emerge thus. The first remit in this consultancy request could focus on *operational* needs. This could involve the consultant and senior managers working together to review the organization's systems, procedures, and policies. The work will be about re-examining the organization's equal opportunity practices in such areas as recruitment, staffing, procedures for grievances, and dismissals. Also included would be a review and appraisal of the organization's diversity initiatives and clear guidance on improvements for change.

The second remit could be a clear brief for consultancy dealing with the organization's *interpersonal* needs. This work will include training concerned with raising general awareness of, and sensitivity to, areas of difference such as culture, race/ethnicity, gender, class, age, sexual orientation, and disability. Important to this area of work would be other concerns, which may include differences in treatment for part-time, seconded, night, and ancillary staff. The focus of such consultancy work would be on issues dealing with conflict resolution and team building, with follow-up sessions for appraisal of improved staff communication and teamwork.

The third remit could address *cultural* needs within the work of the organization. Consultancy can facilitate both (a) the work of appraising acceptable and unacceptable practices that are condoned in the running of the organization's day to day life, for example, acceptance of certain jokes about certain groups, and (b) the widening of knowledge about diverse client groups and their needs, through research, ongoing continuing professional development (CPD), and the diversification of the organization's own staff team.

The fourth remit could centre on the work of addressing *clinical/professional* needs. Training would focus on transcultural counselling and groupwork practice, or addressing issues of diversity in the clinical context. Consultancy can help practitioners to deepen their awareness of issues that facilitate cross-cultural confidence and competence. This activity will have a direct effect on the quality of therapeutic service delivery and in building the practitioner's cross-cultural competence to work with issues of difference.

As described above, delineation of the original organizations remit enables separation of the various organizational tasks and the emergence of clear and specific headings with which to work. A reasonably simple task it may seem; however, it remains a puzzle how such distinct areas are so often fused and treated as one and the same task. A possible explanation for this phenomenon may lie in the fact that the terms Equal Opportunity and Diversity are often reduced to mean one thing: dealing with race only. Because race is a highly misunderstood concept and one that engenders anxiety, negativity, and irrational fear, engaging with this agenda can become problematic for organizations. To engage can be experienced as psychic intrusion and, as Fanon (1986) suggests, such discomfort can lead to irrational thinking. Psychologically speaking, when we feel besieged by external impingements, the natural tendency is to defend against attack. "Splitting", a well-known Kleinian concept, is a common defence mechanism against feelings of being overwhelmed or invaded. It best describes the mental process of separating off the engulfing whole into part objects as a way of defending against the fear of annihilation. The whole then is not allowed to remain separate and intact; rather, it can only be related to in split-off part-object terms. This dynamic can be seen to be operating in certain cultural prejudices about different others. For example, gay people may be viewed solely in terms of their sexuality, that is, promiscuous sexual objects and not as whole beings possessing wider aspects to their identity. Their sexuality is split off to become the only important cultural signifier about this group. Likewise, black men can be objectified solely in terms of their physicality (a threatening sexuality), and not held in mind as being capable of having intellectual capabilities or qualities of gentleness and an intellect. Again, this is the splitting off of the whole object and relating to black men in part-object terms.

Organizations that unwittingly merge very different aspects of their remit by *bundling* very distinct organizational needs and relating to them as one and the same might be guilty of the aforementioned phenomenon. On the other hand, they might also engage in splitting (separating off) multi-dimensional aspects of the diversity remit and trying to deal with the whole challenge in part-object terms.

These defensive processes can also be observed in everyday responses to difference, illustrated by familiar sayings such as, "I don't see people's colour, I treat everyone the same"; "I don't care if you are black, green, purple, or yellow, you are just a human being in my eyes". No matter how honourable the intent of such statements, the effect will always be received as putdowns that deny the other individuality and uniqueness.

Moving on to the second example, of "killing time", the organization's resistance towards engaging in diversity initiatives can be equated with a person's attitude towards authority figures, that is, a negative reaction to being taken over and controlled. If the person has experienced excessively critical authority figures, or been made to feel powerless, a dismissive attitude towards time may result. Many organizations seeking diversity consultancy have experienced pressures from the outside, for example, from funding bodies, a changing cultural climate, and politically vocal members within the organization. Such pressures can be experienced as oppressive and threatening. An employer's grudging lending of time to diversity challenges may be the result, with defensive posturing and the creation of superficial culture of political correctness. Killing time sabotages genuine efforts to engage in the real work of establishing effective antidiscriminatory practice. The consultant can enable this important work by facilitating understanding of these unconscious processes and establishing an atmosphere of collaboration. Remembering that the consultancy at no point belongs to the consultant is critical, and, for these reasons, laying the groundwork for group ownership is also crucial.

Laying the groundwork

Plans for diversity consultancy should involve examination of the organization's strengths, weaknesses, and challenges. A consultant can be hired to conduct this initial assessment to identify a more comprehensive needs assessment programme. The internal needs assessment will undoubtedly reveal a number of priorities and issues for the organization to address, which will be differentiated under the headings of operational, interpersonal, cultural, and clinical/professional, as previously introduced in the heading "Blurring the focus". Employing the same consultant to undertake the work of the whole project may offer continuity, but various needs areas may require different specialist input. Few consultants, in my experience, are able to deliver the full comprehensive package, and, therefore, organizations should be cautioned to invest wisely and according to the consultant's effectiveness and track record.

Written contracts should be an agreed aspect of all consultancy work, as they help to clarify organization goals, objectives, and scope of the work to be undertaken. A written proposal from a consultant provides a good start in evaluating their interest. Contracts should give an indication of the approach employed by the consultant to meet the organization's goals and objectives. Consultants should encourage training agendas to be shaped by the whole team, rather than prescribed by managers and executive committees. The consultant may choose to ask for homework in the form of pre-questionnaires, or request "live" case material to be brought into the training for more immediate and direct learning. Pre-questionnaires form a useful tool for gauging the true nature of staff's views, feelings, and present difficulties. The information may help shape the programme in a more realistic way and identify where "hotspots" are located. As already mentioned, ownership of the programme by the whole team will have the most positive impact in the long term.

Addressing dynamics in black–white relationships

The backdrop of racism

In all cross-cultural encounters, differences inevitably influence the backdrop and nature of the relationship. Such differences need not be a problem, but they invariably pose difficulties in everyday encounters and daily interactions. Within the context of organizations, diversity consultancy can be helpful in addressing these cultural differences while celebrating areas of similarities and commonality. Evidence suggests that, in the UK, religious practices of the more pernicious kind and institutional racism are currently two of the more difficult and politically explosive issues being confronted. Their sensitive nature tends to provoke stronger feelings and stir up much controversy in our present climate. Despite this reality, it would be true to say that changing attitudes and reviewed legislation in the UK are slowly succeeding in raising awareness of social and political injustices. Progress, however, is still very slow, and problems of inequality and discrimination continue to be everyday experiences for British black and ethnic minorities.

Against the above backdrop, there are personal challenges in the pursuit of acquiring deeper cross-cultural confidence. One such challenge is being able to deal with all that is thrown up by *the internal racist*. This is a concept put forward by Davids (1992), who suggests that the impact of psychic internal organization is of such a nature that it enables a majority group people to fix a minority group in a rigid stereotypical position, both internally and externally. Davids purports that the maintenance of such fixed boundaries between black and white individuals can, for example, prevent whites from having to face the primitive infantile parts of themselves, as well as the shame and guilt of an unpleasant historical colonial past. Organizational diversity consultancy can be effective in confronting these themes by enabling individuals to examine their own personal value and beliefs systems, and, furthermore, discover effective ways of challenging intentional and unintentional discriminatory practices in the workplace.

The impact of race, ethnicity, and culture plays a critical and significant role in all therapeutic work with racial minorities. Organizational diversity initiatives often present major challenges for providing adequate and culturally sensitive services to Black, Asian, and Minority Ethnic (BAME) groups. Organizations that are striving for cultural competence in this area require both a deep understanding of the influence and impact of racism and racial prejudice on these groups, together with a committed approach to integrating issues of diversity in the mainstream of the organization's life.

The following themes are important for organizations to address in providing a culturally sensitive therapeutic service to BME groups.

The "mark of oppression" as pathology

Stereotypical attitudes towards black and ethic minorities can influence the nature and quality of service offered. Assumptions that hold, for example, that black people are blighted by racial oppression and are, therefore, scarred victims, will only serve to pathologize black clients as people who are ill or needing "special" treatment or dispensation. Emotional difficulties may easily be perceived in medical or psychiatric terms, rather than accurately understood and assessed as real presentations of dis-ease and distress. Thomas and Sillen (1972) suggest that such dangerous thinking can contribute to a generalized view about black people as suffering the "mark of oppression", a term which implies that BAME clients are deficient and damaged in some irreversible way. Such perceptions can severely limit the establishment of a *true* relationship with clients from these groups and, in turn, damage the organization's ability to provide appropriate cross-cultural services to the community. Evidence of such damage are seen in the higher rates of black people being given custodial sentences and put through the psychiatric system, as opposed to being offered psychotherapeutic help and other psychological interventions.

The illusion of "colour blindness"

"Colour blindness" is, in many ways, the reverse of "the mark of oppression". Within the illusion of colour blindness, racial difference is fleetingly acknowledged, or not at all. Blackness, as an example, is viewed in either problematic ways or as being unnecessary to the concept of personal identity. Such responses indicate denial of individual differences and a tendency to conflate uniqueness in humanity. Colour blindness overlooks socio-economic and political realities of black and minority ethnic individuals and communities, and can lead to a belief that race does not matter. Statements such as "I don't see your colour"; "It doesn't matter to me whether you are black, white, green, or purple, it's the person that counts"; "Anyone can adopt a black child . . . love is all it needs" are all indications of a denial and exclusion of racial and cultural differences. Although such statements may be meant in good faith and reflect cultural naïveté rather than intentional harm, this does not make them any less offensive or damaging to the recipient.

A public example and interesting twist on the theme of colour blindness may also be observed in the way particular sections of society here in the UK have discussed America's presidential elections and the relatively recently elected Barack Obama. Black people and some sections of white society appear to have no reservation in perceiving this president as black. Indeed, the event has gone down in history as momentous and ground-breaking precisely for this reason. However, at the time of writing this chapter,

UK discourse continues to comment on Obama as mixed-race, thus reinforcing the notion that he is not black. The apparent preoccupation with Obama's racial identity appears almost as an unconscious wish to make him *less black*, raising further discussion about what constitutes blackness and how we how we interpret public and private racial identity.

Cultural competence as a goal of diversity consultancy is not just about consciousness raising and mere intent, but a willingness and commitment to be proactive in the pursuit of change and inclusivity.

Understanding the black "defensive" persona

Grier and Cobbs (1986), in their book *Black Rage*, offer a distinction between healthy cultural paranoia and pathological states in black people. Healthy cultural paranoia is regarded as a cautious, guarded, and watchful stance that a black person may adopt in their interactions with white people in predominantly white settings. This stance can often be misinterpreted as having a suspicious disposition, or even being clinically paranoid. Grier and Cobbs suggest that this "defensive" stance may result from experiences of societal racism and personal discrimination. In such circumstances, black people develop high levels of mistrust—a way of always questioning and protecting themselves from further hurt. Mistrust in this context can spill over into all interactions, including therapeutic situations, and can lead to problems when black people are seeking help from the white medical establishment. Caution and mistrust may present as defensiveness. and there may be a resistance to engaging therapeutically. Lack of cultural awareness and understanding of such cultural presentations can lead to inaccurate labelling of minorities as presenting with pathological behaviour and abnormal mental functioning. Emotional and psychological distress may be perceived as illness, and social dis-ease may be seen in terms of disease. Such harmful labels contribute to high levels of mistrust and increasing dividedness of feelings. We know that repeated experiences of hurt could naturally lead to higher levels of vigilance and sensitivity. Therefore, guardedness, or defensive posturing, observed in some black people may well be a "normal" reaction to this phenomenon, and one that needs to be understood in terms of the perceived and often real threat of being hurt. Learning how to distinguish between these subtle presentations can help to prevent the perpetuation of this form of damaging stereotyping.

Defensiveness in intercultural relations is not confined to black and minority individuals. White clients and white workers also show mistrust and caution in relating to the black or different ethnic other. In such instances, this behaviour appears to stem from irrational fear of the unknown and unfamiliar and subsequent avoidance of these differences. Intellectualization rationalization, repression, and displacement are all defensive structures that can be employed in this process. Familiar statements such as, "They don't really understand us", and "They are not like us", are common responses to these difficulties and, in turn, can block initiatives for cultural inclusivity and good relations in organizations.

Indifference, as another aspect of this form of defensiveness, is, in my view, the most pernicious, because its impact can render the different other insignificant and a non-person. Indifference in workplace settings can be observed towards the minority member who gets singled out for the cold shoulder treatment. The "victim" who experiences this may be left feeling isolated, disappointed, and let down. When indifference becomes an established part of the whole organizational culture, the "victim" can gradually be made to feel invisible and worthless.

Grier and Cobbs (1986) remind us of yet another kind of defensive tendency in black and minority ethnic people, where the individual adopts a submissive and over-compliant persona when interacting with the majority culture. In these instances, low racial self-esteem will have played a part in eroding feelings of self-worth and personal entitlement. The "defensive" stance is a reaction against internalizing negative and inferior beliefs about oneself, together with the impact of other cultural narcissistic injuries.

Working with the "internal oppressor"

The internal oppressor (Alleyne, 2004, 2005a,b), a clinical concept borne out of my doctoral research, contributes towards deepening understanding of hidden dimensions of internalized oppression and racial identity wounding. Its relevance to diversity consultancy is crucial, and although the focus of research was confined to the black experience, its outcome clearly has relevance to other minority group experiences.

The internal oppressor can be conceptualized as an internal adversary influencing black people's struggles and drives for actualization of their full and innate hybrid potential. Black people's struggles are not just concerned with external impingements from racism and racial oppression, but also from internal challenges affecting a sense of self and existence. While there is some recognition of mass-scale racial oppression and its consequences on the psyche, little attention is given to the internal adversary—the internal oppressor and its effect on personal autonomy. As Bach (1985) stated, the inner enemy is as much a formidable foe as the most manipulative (or oppressive) of associates. This profound statement is a reminder that it is equally important to permit challenge and reflection of what "the victim" might also be bringing to the difficult encounter, as well acknowledge the impact of social wounding and the recovery from these diminishing environmental experiences.

What is the nature of the internal oppressor?

Much is known and written about internalized oppression (Freire, 1970; hooks, 1989, 1996; Lipsky, 1987; Lorde, 1984), seen as the process of absorbing negative values and beliefs of the oppressor. This process invariably leads to self-hate, low self-esteem, the disowning of one's group, and other complex defensive behaviours and attitudes.

As distinct from the process of internalized oppression, the internal oppressor is an aspect of the self that functions as an inhibitor to personal and collective progress.

Akbar (1996) and DeGruy-Leary (2005) conceptualize the internal holding of the legacy of slavery and its effects in terms of a "post-traumatic slave syndrome". The theory suggests that centuries of the painful history of slavery, followed by systemic racism and oppression, have resulted in multi-generational adaptive behaviours, some of which have been positive and reflective of resilience, and others that are detrimental and destructive.

The internal oppressor is not just concerned with historical baggage, but includes other factors that shape personal makeup, such as personal prejudices, projections, narcissistic injuries, and unresolved family difficulties where power and domination feature. The internal oppressor is reawakened when it is in contact with an external oppressive situation, such as present-day racism that is either real, perceived, or a mixture of both. In these circumstances, historical wounds are reopened, compounding the effects of the here and now wounding experience, thereby re-wounding the sufferer, who is now doubly affected by these negative experiences. The reopening of historical wounds may explain why some apparently small hurts can be deeply felt as damaging. Diversity consultancy can utilize this concept in very sensitive ways to help teams and managers understand hidden dimensions in racial and cultural conflict within mixed teams.

Diversity consultancy with groups at different stages of development

Meeting varying levels of cross-cultural awareness and abilities in work groups can present special challenges for the consultant in their preparation for tailoring effective training programmes. The following subheadings describe four developmental stages for working with different levels of group functioning, and they highlight challenges that can be met at each stage. These developmental stages can very much mirror aspects of childhood development and its emergence into adulthood.

Stage 1. The underdeveloped group

In this stage, group members are generally very naïve about issues of diversity, culture, and racism in particular. They can vacillate between being highly motivated and complacent in addressing these challenges. Some participants might be very keen and eager, while others may be highly anxious and more reticent. Generally, Stage 1 group members are more task orientated, often exhibiting poor listening skills because of their inexperience. The consultant is steered into adopting more of an educative role and, thus, offering more directives. Facilitation needs to incorporate a higher input of didactic teaching that requires much time to clarify diversity and equal opportunity terminology. Full explanation of the list, covering terms such as heterosexism, ethnocentricism, xenophobia, racism, and racial prejudice is necessary. Stage 1 activities will include simple, non-threatening exercises geared towards participants examining their own identity through exploration of their own cultural beliefs and value systems. Self-reflective work is aimed at helping the group to be more acquainted with issues of the cultural and the racial self, something many white individuals take for granted because of being in the majority culture. These rudimentary exercises facilitate an understanding of crucial 'micro' processes in working with diversity issues and they build strong foundations for the ongoing work in this challenging area.

Stage 2. The ambivalent group

In Stage 2, group members are not new to challenges of working with issues of difference and diversity. Many would have had a previous experience of diversity training and, as a result, enter subsequent trainings with caution, mistrust, and apprehension. Arriving late for sessions, requesting unnecessary clarification of the instructions given by the facilitator, and *killing off* valuable training time by reflecting endlessly on previous negative diversity consultancy experiences, are just a few of the ways the group may show its ambivalence and rebelliousness. The consultant may also meet complaints about group members having to relinquish other "important" priorities to attend the diversity training and, as a consequence, have to deal with their requests to leave early. At Stage 2, there is often the tendency for minority members to be singled out for the group's projections, as well as being pushed into being spokespersons for their racial or cultural group. In such situations, the consultant's role is to employ a no-blame approach to the consultancy and provide effective paternal, as well as maternal, containment. The paternal metaphor in this instance is one that provides structure, task, boundaries, authority, and reality. These are key building blocks geared towards helping the consultant construct a reliable setting in which containment of the group's anxiety is more likely. The consultant, therefore, is not a sounding board, but an active partisan who can provide holding and empathize with the individual as well as the larger group's needs. Confessions of previous negative training experiences should be given reasonable air time to help restore trust and calm nerves. New learning is more likely to take place when such material is ventilated and sufficient trust has been re-established in the individual member and the group as a whole. Introducing audiovisual aids to address specific diversity challenges can be very helpful at this stage, as well as using role plays and other challenging exercises to facilitate learning.

Stage 3. The experimenting group

Groups at Stage 3 dive headfirst into the programme and show genuine interest in pro-minority concerns. Group members confront issues more freely and talk about their achievements and struggles in working with diversity issues, some of which can include group members having to deal with historical guilt and shame. White majority members may even discuss issues of alienation by other whites who do not share their world views. In such an open group setting, there is sometimes a tendency to idealize minority cultures and denigrate the white majority. This can become a problem if left unchecked. A pro-minority stance can stymie movement within a group and collude with underlying uncertainties that may be present in individual and the group itself. Idealization of minorities must be challenged, as it can be a defence against cultural superiority, examples of which might be expressed thus: "Chinese people are geniuses at innovation, but their original ideas are always stolen from others" (an implication that the Chinese are cultural pirates); or, "I envy minority cultures that are more spontaneous and open, but at the end of the day, you can't beat the English reserve" (an implication that the English reserve is more desirable and respectable); or, "I think it's healthy that other cultures can grieve so openly, but there is a particular dignity in our stiff upper lip approach" (an implication that open grief is undignified and improper). These barely veiled "yes-but" *insults* need gentle challenging in order to facilitate careful reflection of the underlying messages. Stage 3 group participants respond well in the main to such constructive criticism and, therefore, make it much easier for the consultant to facilitate more robust discourse with the topics. A varied programme involving role-plays, working with "live" case material from the participants work settings, utilizing scenarios from the consultant's own repertoire, can all make for a rich programme of diversity consultancy. The consultant can go on to introduce more complex themes of power and powerlessness, internalized oppression, cultural shame, racism as projection, etc., as relevant areas in further challenge towards deepening cross-cultural knowledge and understanding.

Stage 4. The mature group

The mature group is a performing working entity that appears more purposeful in meeting the task of the organization. Members listen more actively, use questions more skilfully and are more cohesive as a group. Members pull together and present as more confident in dealing with the unknown and unfamiliar. The group looks to itself for guidance and devises its own procedures for working things out, often in an autonomous and creative way. Where there was once fear, anxiety, and conflict in dealing with issues of difference and diversity, there is now tolerance, calm, and confidence. The group can be more creative in pursuing the organization's goals. The consultant's role with Stage 4 group participants is to assist them with their needs and by offering creative facilitation, structure, and guidance. Stage 4 group members make it their business to challenge all forms of oppression, not necessarily what is fashionable or "in" at the time. As a consequence, their motto supports the statement: *if you are not part of the solution, you are part of the problem.*

Conclusion

This chapter has discussed some subtle considerations in organizational diversity consultancy from a psychodynamic perspective. Psychodynamic thinking implies a dynamic, interactive process of going about change, as opposed to a static or linear appearance of making adjustments. This chapter has argued that effective diversity consultancy must include attention to both "micro" (internal and unconscious) and "macro" (external and conscious) processes. I have chosen to focus mainly on "micro" processes and the more subtle aspects of black–white dynamics operating in organizational workplace contexts. The chapter has addressed pre-transference issues, which prepare the consultant and the organization for engaging in the challenge of achieving cross-cultural effectiveness and inclusivity. Specific themes are presented and discussed, which lay the groundwork for deepening such knowledge. I have identified the pitfalls and rewards of working with different level group challenges in this area. The chapter's overall message highlights the fact that "difference" matters, and the investment in working with its challenges is paramount. The chapter also emphasizes the fact that subtle "micro" issues need just as much attention as the more obvious and public strategies ("macro" issues) organizations invest in to meet the important requirements of the diversity challenge. The chapter's theme reminds us that difference is ever present in the workplace and diversity consultancy can be an effective way of keeping its vibrancy alive in an effective, healthy, and positive way.

References

Akbar, N. (1996). *Breaking the chains of psychological slavery*. Tallahassee, FL: Mind Productions.

Alleyne. A. (2004). The internal oppressor and black identity wounding. *Counselling and Psychotherapy Journal, 15*(10): 48–50.

Alleyne, A. (2005a). The internal oppressor- the veiled companion of external racial oppression. *UKCP—The Psychotherapist, 26*: 10–13.

Alleyne, A. (2005b). Invisible injuries and silent witnesses: the shadow of racial oppression in workplace contexts. *Psychodyanamic Practice, 11*(3): 283–299.

Bach, G. R. (1985). *The Inner Enemy: How to Fight Fair with Yourself.* New York: Berkley Publishing Group.

Curry, A. (1964). Myth, transference and the black psychotherapist. *International Review of Psychoanalysis, 45*: 89–120.

Davids, M. F. (1992). The cutting edge of racism: an object relations view. *Bulletin of the British Psychoanalytic Society, 28*(11): 19–29.

DeGruy-Leary, J. (2005). *Post-Traumatic Slave Syndrome: America's Legacy of Enduring Injury & Healing.* Milwaukee, OR: Uptone Press.

Fanon, F. (1986). *Black Skin, White Masks.* London: Pluto Press.

Freire, P. (1970). *Pedagogy of the Oppressed*. New York: Continuum.

Grier, W. H., & Cobbs, P. M. (1969). *Black Rage*. London: Cape.

hooks, B. (1989). *Talking Back: Thinking Feminist, Thinking Black*. Boston, MA: South End Press.

hooks, B. (1996). *Killing Rage: Ending Racism*. Harmondsworth: Penguin.

Lipsky, S. (1987). *Internalised Racism*. Seattle, WA: Rational Island.

Lorde, A. (1984). *Sister Outsider*. Trumansburg, NY: Cross Press.

Thomas, A., & Sillen, S. (1972). *Racism and Psychiatry*. New York: Brunner/Mazel.

INDEX